Empathy
and
Confrontation
in
Pastoral Care

THEOLOGY AND PASTORAL CARE SERIES
edited by
Don S. Browning

RALPH L. UNDERWOOD

Empathy and Confrontation in Pastoral Care

Don S. Browning, *editor*

THEOLOGY AND PASTORAL CARE

FORTRESS PRESS
PHILADELPHIA

Library of Congress Cataloging-in-Publication Data

Underwood, Ralph L.
  Empathy and confrontation in pastoral care.

  (Theology and pastoral care)
  Bibliography: p.
  1. Pastoral psychology. 2. Communication (Theology)
  3. Empathy—Religious aspects—Christianity. I. Title
  II. Series: Theology and pastoral care series.
  BV4012.U53 1986   253.5   85–47722
  ISBN 0–8006–1737–1

1727D85   Printed in the United States of America   1–1737

Dedicated to the Memory of
Friend and Colleague
Ross Denison Dunn
January 15, 1937–May 1, 1984

Contents

Series Foreword

The purpose of the Theology and Pastoral Care series is four-fold: to present to ministers and church leaders a series of readable books that will (1) retrieve the theological and ethical foundations of the Judeo-Christian tradition for pastoral care, (2) develop lines of communication between pastoral theology and the other disciplines of theology, (3) create an ecumenical dialogue on pastoral care, and (4) do this in such a way as to affirm yet go beyond the recent preoccupation of pastoral care with secular psychotherapy and the other social sciences.

The books in this series are written by authors who are well acquainted with psychology, psychotherapy, and the other social sciences. All of them affirm the importance of these disciplines for modern societies and for ministry in particular. But each of them sees the disciplines as potentially destructive of human values unless they are guided in their practical application by tested religious and ethical traditions. To retrieve the best of the Judeo-Christian tradition for the church's care and counseling is a challenging intellectual task—a task to which few writers in the area of pastoral care have attended with sufficient thoroughness. This series addresses this task out of a broad ecumenical stance, with all of the authors taking an ecumenical approach to theology. In addition to a vigorous investigation of Protestant resources, there will be specific books dealing with pastoral care in Judaism and Catholicism.

We hope that the series will help ministers and church leaders view afresh the theological and ethical foundations of care and counseling. All of the books will have a practical dimension to them, but even more important than that, they will help us all see the matter of care and counseling differently. In light of the last thirty years of writing in this field, some of the books will seem startlingly different. Some will need to be read and pondered with care. But I have little doubt that the books in the series will make a profound and lasting impact upon the way we understand and practice our care for one another.

In *Empathy and Confrontation in Pastoral Care,* Ralph Underwood has given us an extremely useful book that brings to practical expression several of the major themes of this series. Many of the earlier books in the series have called for approaches to pastoral care that require a wider range of behaviors on the part of the minister than have usually been associated with pastoral care in recent decades. The minister cannot range from moral inquiry to empathic understanding to guidance to consolation to active support, with a narrow range of verbal responses. As important as it was to encourage ministers to listen and to reflect back in Rogerian fashion the messages and feelings of the people they cared for, a rigid and ritualistic use of the Rogerian empathic response was defeating to the goals of good care and counseling.

Ralph Underwood is a professor at Austin Presbyterian Seminary. Before accepting this position, he had several years of experience within the context of Granger Westberg's well-known Wholistic Health programs. Professor Underwood convincingly argues that there is a role for both empathy *and* confrontation in pastoral care. The common element that holds the two modalities of care together is the highly crucial quality of respect. Respect is fundamental to the communication of empathy. But it is even more fundamental to the communication of confrontation and judgment. Through the category of respect, Ralph Underwood has brought together the contemporary emphasis on client-centered sensitivity and the older Reformed and Catholic understanding of pastoral care as moral guidance and spiritual direction.

Professor Underwood understands the role of metaphors in the ministry of the church. He nominates the metaphor of the

Word as the central organizing metaphor for the pastoral care ministry of the church. But in addition to having this interesting theological focus, the book is extremely practical and highly useful to anyone attempting to develop a more flexible style of pastoral care—one relevant to the more complicated models of care that the books in this series seem to be requiring for the future of pastoral care.

DON S. BROWNING

Acknowledgments

I wish to thank Don S. Browning for his able and creative leadership in making possible the series on Theology and Pastoral Care, and for his encouragement and guidance in the preparation of this study of empathy and confrontation in pastoral ministry.

Other readers whose comments have been especially helpful include Dr. James L. Mayfield, District Superintendent in the Southwest Texas Conference of the United Methodist Church, Dr. Prescott H. Williams, Jr., Professor of Old Testament Languages and Archaeology at Austin Presbyterian Theological Seminary, and the late Seward Hiltner. I regret that I have not been able to incorporate all of their suggestions in this volume, but they have contributed to it and their wisdom will influence my future endeavors.

Dorothy Andrews is the most efficient typist I ever have known, and so I happily credit her for her marvelous help in preparation of the manuscript.

Finally, I thank The University of Texas at Austin, which through the offices of Gerhard J. Fonken, Vice-President for Academic Affairs and Research, named me Visiting Scholar in the spring term of 1983. At the University, Ira Iscoe, Professor of Psychology and Education and Director of the Institute of Human Development and Family Studies, provided me space to write and was a gracious host and colleague in this endeavor.

CHAPTER 1

Ministry as Communication

The purpose of this study is to explore the relationship between empathy and confrontation in the context of pastoral care. Frequently, the contrast between these modes of relating has been heightened to the degree that ministers feel that they must choose one style of communication or the other. No common bond is recognized. Indeed, they are distinct. Empathy educes clarity if not wisdom from the person being helped, whereas confrontation demands that one recognize what one has been denying. Empathy is based on the possibility of harmony if not unity between two persons; confrontation aims to make use of tension between persons for creative challenge. How can one ministry embody both styles of communication? Let us consider this question in terms of an incident in the life of a minister whom I shall call Roger Babcock. He is a minister who was trained in seminary when nondirective counseling was emphasized. For him empathy became both a technique and an approach to ministry.

Pastor Babcock had come from the home of a middle-aged widow, Mrs. Smith. He was frustrated and puzzled because he was aware of an uneasiness on his part that had made their conversation stiff and awkward at points. He had had one quarter of Clinical Pastoral Education and was committed to examining his ministry with a critical eye. Reflecting on his relationship with this parishioner, he recalled that it had been more than a year since her husband had died. Lately each visit mirrored the previous one: she exuded depression and spoke of an emptiness and hopelessness that blanketed her life. She never expressed concern about her teen-age son. Pastor Babcock had observed the son's development over the year—a youth still subdued occasionally, but more and more active in the youth program of the church and affirmative in spirit. Viewing grief as a process with stages, Pastor Babcock saw himself as a facilitator whose presence and understanding could help this woman work through her loss. He had been empathic to the best of his ability and could remember moments when he felt that his ministry was meaningful to her, and to himself as one who had been allowed to share another's suffering. Still, he feared that she was not coming to terms with her loss but might be feeling a self-pity that could become an orientation toward life. This possibility disturbed him, and he found himself wrestling with the following questions: What does being a facilitator mean in this situation? Is empathy the pastoral task even though it seems that no new depth or direction is educed? Should I confront her or will doing so shift the unwritten rules of our relationship and undercut the trust she has in me? Suddenly Pastor Babcock felt that he lacked a clear understanding of his role and felt uncertain about the ways in which he might be helpful.

Because of this incident Pastor Babcock began to explore the relation of empathy and confrontation in his pastoral ministry. To do this he had to raise questions concerning the overall meaning of his ministry and the particulars by which a vision or model of ministry is constructed.

In order to examine the relationship between empathy and confrontation in pastoral ministry, this study intends to address the concerns of pastors like Mr. Babcock who struggle to attain clarity of purpose and a sense of competence in their ministry. That is, in the course of interpreting the relation of empathy and confrontation, I hope to enlarge the capacity of pastors to understand how basic meaning guides concrete methods and how in turn specific strategies express a vision of ministry. In other words, the purpose of this project is to promote an understanding of how meaning and method are related in pastoral care, through an analysis of the place of empathy and confrontation.

This problem should be of interest to pastors who have been

trained in nondirective counseling or listening, as well as pastors who have been exposed to a wide variety of counseling techniques. For example, cognitive-behavioral modification techniques make up a family of strategies. One way to summarize the significance of the many techniques that have emerged to shape pastoral ministry "beyond empathy" is to note how most of them enable pastors to be confrontive and challenging in their ministry with people. How these methods relate to empathy has for the most part not been addressed. For some ministers these techniques in effect take the place of empathy. For others these methods are strategies that work in certain situations, while empathy is a method that works in other situations. This study explores the relationship of empathic and confrontive modes of communication as well as the place of both in the context of pastoral ministry.

This book then is addressed in the main to ministers in parish settings who are not specialists in pastoral care and counseling but who want practical guidance for the informal situations in which they are expected to be of assistance to persons in their faith, personal development, and daily problems and who want to be able to draw on that guidance from a clear image of their ministry. I hope that this endeavor will also be a resource for seminary students who want to anticipate some of the situations they will face in their parish ministry and want to learn how a model of professional self-understanding shapes practice. Pastoral care and counseling specialists who look for resources to interpret the relation of their work to ordained ministry as a whole, who seek ways to articulate bases for their accountability to both church and society, and who desire to review and assess their work from the perspective of the meaning and methods of communication in pastoral conversations may wish to examine this study.

METHOD: FROM ONE TO MANY

The reader may have noticed how traditional Pastor Babcock's approach to pastoral work is. After all, in his ministry he has been relying consistently on (though he has begun to question) empathy. Years ago when I was a seminary student, the nondirective,

Rogerian approach to counseling dominated the field—in part, because it was viewed as a safe method for persons with limited training in psychological disciplines. At any rate, empathy was both technique and orientation. Pastoral education advocated one approach to people and one set of concrete descriptions of how that approach was to be put into practice. Now a bewildering array of techniques is available to pastors thanks to a psychological "populism" that aims to teach everyone in our culture how to cope. Popular psychology has influenced pastors, their parishioners, and theological education. Consequently, pastoral care often is characterized by ad hoc attempts to try vast arrays of techniques in order to see what works in each immediate situation. A pastor may, for example, try Transactional Analysis techniques for a time and then switch to a rational-emotive approach until the psychological grapevine tells him or her of another method that can be tried after attendance at one readily available workshop.

I admit that the above characterization is unfair. A kinder interpretation might describe current pastoral ministry as alive and experimental, which indeed it is. The wider openness and diversity that mark pastoral care today are evidence of its vitality. I do not wish to belittle this evidence of vitality. I fully appreciate the parish pastor's desire to be of practical help to people. At the same time, the present situation provokes several concerns. How do such diverse techniques relate to the pastoral role? At what point do people begin to relate to pastors as if they were secular counselors rather than ministers of the Word and Sacraments? To raise such questions is not to counsel pious rejection of psychological wisdom and knowledge from any source. Rather, it would be prudent to examine how various techniques may advance or hinder one's pastoral purpose, however unwittingly.

Another question can be raised: How does the Christian faith inform the use of the various methods being used today in pastoral care? Pastors should be aware that most methods propounded in the current wave of psychological "populism" emerge from some normative position. For example, pastors in the Reformed tradition who study the promise and limitations of rational-emotive therapy as applied to pastoral ministry may discover that they have been drawn to this approach in part because it has confidence in the power of cognitions and beliefs. On the other hand, they can discern that the rational-emotional approach labels certain personal beliefs irrational and others rational on the basis of the Stoic assumptions that underlie this therapy. At this point pastors have the task of relating their understanding of Christian faith in constructive and critical ways to the question of which beliefs are worthy and which are not.

A final concern that has not been resolved by the plethora of techniques available for interpersonal helping is expressed in this question: How can we as pastors enhance accountability for our competence in pastoral care? I believe that we are letting ourselves off the hook if we do not declare and specify what we are responsible for and in what we profess to be competent as pastors who care for the individuals who bring their personal celebrations and problems to us. While the superfluity of psychological methods that impact pastoral practice has introduced a greater degree of detail, it is not evident that a greater degree of methodological stability has been achieved.

These questions can be addressed equally to ministers who, like Pastor Babcock, have relied on one method and to those who try whatever works. The concerns about pastoral purpose that the questions represent can be translated into criteria for evaluating techniques and methods. First, despite the undesirability of the ad hoc character in the strategies of many pastors, methods and techniques should be readily applicable to the informal situations in which people reach out to pastors. Parking lot and coffee shop conversations, for instance, are typically brief and not formally structured by an appointment hour. Second, methods should fit within the pastor's self-concept and role. Third, whatever the immediate source of a method, it should hold up under constructive and critical examination from the side of Christian faith. Finally, the method should be sufficiently concrete that it provides adequate data for accountability.

To summarize, since the relation of empathy to theological and pastoral interests has been examined with some care, pastors who rely on this approach have resources that help them to articulate the integral relation of their methodology to their pastoral vision. The problem that challenges them is the question of the adequacy of their method to the variety of situations their pastoral care entails. How different is the case of the pastors who experiment with and develop many techniques. Like most utilitarians, they do not have a sense of limits. Rather, voluntary strategies can be devised for virtually any situation. Here two questions give expression to the problem of integrity: What principles limit the proliferation of techniques? How do techniques relate to basic purpose? I hope to examine the relationship of empathy and confrontation in a manner that will address both questions, for the two approaches reflect the horns of the dilemma so many pastors experience: either they constrict the range of their adequacy in order to gain a sense of integrity or they expand the range of their responses to the human concerns brought to them to the point where continuity and even a sense of direction in what they do are lost.

A MODEL OF MINISTRY REVISITED
Ministry of the Word

In order to explore the concerns and questions introduced above, I plan to relate a model of ministry as the communication of the gospel, to a set of methods in pastoral conversations. The familiar form of this model, which Avery Dulles labels the "herald" model of ministry,[1] requires reinterpretation. The communication of the gospel entails the image of the herald but is richer and more diverse than this image suggests.

The model of ministry as communication of the Word of God emphasizes the fundamental significance of all communication in ministry, including the ordained ministry of the church. Ministry is grounded in God's love and regard for human life. Divine esteem for human life is dramatically disclosed in the Christ, through whom we recognize God's empathy with human suffering and God's caring confrontation. We do not merit this esteem. Rather, the high value God places on human life is the reality that initiates divine-human communication and evokes mutual esteem among people. In turn, this esteem or valuing energizes and guides human communication. Applied to empathy and confrontation as moments in human communication, this model leads us to the thesis that both empathy and confrontation—when sound in spirit and right in moral principle—are expressions of respect. Thus respect is the key to understanding empathy and confrontation in pastoral ministry. I hope to show the importance of this concept for an understanding of ministry as communication of the gospel.

Metaphor

In order to envision the many meanings of ministry of the Word, I propose to analyze the image of the Word as a root metaphor. The ministry of the Word is a root metaphor that cannot be reduced to the prophetic tradition and preaching.

By a root metaphor I mean that "ministry of the Word" or "the Word" are references to a basic image that gives us our understanding and theory of what ministry is. The image precedes the understanding and generates the theory. A root metaphor is no mere illustration that we construct and use at will. The root metaphor—in this instance, "the Word" as metaphor— sets before us a vision of ministry.

The common-sense approach to a metaphor is to think of it as a convenient illustration for an idea. The illustration or analogy often enables the one who is considering a concept to grasp it and its implications. This is so because the metaphor introduces an element of familiarity. In contrast to this common understanding of the metaphorical, root metaphor theory suggests that there are some metaphors that do far more than illustrate thoughts that precede them. Rather, certain fundamental metaphors precede thinking, constitute it, and generate ways of thinking. Max Black argues that all scientific concepts, no matter how precise, ensconce a metaphorical image and that scientific theories are elaborations of metaphors that spark the imagination. Following this and similar accounts in the philosophy of science, T. S. Kuhn propounds the theory that science proceeds by basic paradigms. Consequently, science may be guided by one paradigm for a period in its development, only for this paradigm to be supplanted in a revolutionary way by the advent of another that gives birth to new research and concepts for empirical discovery. Stephen Pepper's *World Hypotheses* tries to show how four key metaphors give shape to the history of philosophical thought in the West.[2]

If this approach to the philosophy of science and philosophy in general has merit, how much more is it pertinent to religious thought and theology. Since thought is based on images, it makes sense to think that various theories of the church's ministry and the role of the ordained minister are guided by metaphors that create thought. It also follows that various theories of pastoral theology and models of pastoral care spring from foundational metaphors. One can then analyze developments in these fields in terms of root metaphors that picture the fundamental insight and sense of direction in the various approaches. The organismic metaphor, for example, informs much pastoral theory that has been responsive to Rogerian theory and research or has emphasized wholeness and the interconnected aspects of a whole, such as a person or a community. One can compare this to the conflict metaphor and model of ministry, which has been influenced by dynamic psychologies, especially since Freud, and accordingly is developed to help ministers be responsive to internal dynamics and the dynamics of interpersonal relationships in pastoral work. The reason pastoral care has not paid extensive attention to behaviorism is that it rejects the mechanistic model of cause and effect that has dominated this approach.

Scripture

To say that the ministry of the Word is a root metaphor that cannot be reduced to the prophetic tradition and to preaching is not to depreciate these forms of ministry, for indeed they model the metaphor. The point is to see that the meaning of ministry of the Word is broader and more diverse than these historic and contemporary forms of ministry suggest. This fact can be acknowledged, however, without our having to ignore the importance of prophetic dimensions of ministry. Indeed, the prophetic element is widely distributed throughout Scripture. The patriarchs and Moses spoke with God—and God spoke with them. We should note here the sense of an intimate dialogue binding the human and the divine together, but this dialogical moment in divine-human communication does not exclude the element of pronouncement, for the people did not believe that they could stand to hear God's speech, and so they relied on Moses to hear and relay God's messages.

Granted the vitality of the prophetic form of the Word, we can fill out the picture by noting the many uses of the Word as metaphor in Scripture. In the New Testament alone, the Word refers to the Old Testament Law, particular Old Testament passages, the will of God as disclosed to his people, the word proclaimed by Jesus, the Christian message, and the Christ of faith.[3] The symbol of the Word arises out of many meanings and undergoes a personification: the Word is Christ; Christ is the Word of God. Henceforth, the meaning of ministry is not limited to anyone's prophetic utterances; it involves who one is and all aspects of one's communication. That is, Christ is the true minister, and our ministry is a matter of Christ's being in us. Our ministry is as varied as the many ways in which Christ may speak to us and through us. Christ's ministry exceeds Jesus's prophetic utterances, for especially through his suffering and exaltation we come to realize that Christ's ministry entails who he is and what he does as well as what he says.

In the Scriptures the metaphorical nature of the Word binds speech and action together. The Old Testament tells of a God who acts and whose actions disclose the meaning of God's relationship with his people. Thus the actions speak. This God speaks and his speaking is recorded in the Law, taught in the wisdom literature, and announced by the prophets. This speaking is an acting, a form of action wherein God establishes and carries forward his covenant. Thus the words accomplish an action and generate events. Vatican II stated the situation this way: "This plan of revelation is realized by deeds and words having an inner unity; the deeds wrought by God in the history of salvation manifest the teaching and the realities signified by the words, while the words proclaim the deeds and clarify the mystery contained in them."[4]

Theory

What difference does the recognition of a root metaphor behind a theoretical approach make? It helps to clarify the origins and directions of any specific theory. Furthermore, because root metaphor theory stresses the surplus of meaning that generates any theory it helps to establish an important understanding and attitude toward theory. An attitude that envisions creative extension of the metaphor is flexible with respect to the metaphor. Awareness of the metaphorical dimension helps to prevent reification. Specifically, I believe that such a metaphorical understanding of the nature of human thought can help to restore the metaphor of the Word to the field of pastoral care. A less literalistic but serious and fundamental understanding of the Word as a metaphor of God's relation to humanity helps us to envision the significance of communication for theology and pastoral care. Understood as a metaphor—not one that we invent or that is a matter of human convention or manipulation, but one that grounds our understanding of God's revelation, action, and covenantal relationship with humanity—the Word can be a vision of what pastoral care is.

One final word about root metaphors and pastoral care models: Metaphors have the power to generate theory that is rooted in Christian Scripture and tradition and to stimulate practical methods in pastoral ministry without being totally exclusive. All such metaphors are found in the scriptural writings. Throughout the history of the church's ministry, now one metaphor, now another, has come to dominance for a time. In advancing the metaphor of the Word, I assume that the time is ripe for its ascendance in pastoral ministry. Now we are ready to move beyond particular limits of how this metaphor is applied. I anticipate that a root metaphor understanding of ministry of the Word has ecumenical and practical potential in the pastoral care of clergy.

PASTORAL CARE AS
COMMUNICATION OF THE GOSPEL

What are the main implications of approaching the question of the relation of empathy and confrontation, by reference to ministry of the Word as the key symbol? I discuss these implications by examining pastoral care as communication of the gospel, the relation of communication to community, the importance of community and communication for character formation, and the place of interpersonal communication competencies in the development of character. These considerations lead to a thesis regarding the relation of empathy and confrontation in pastoral care.

At this point, as an initial step, this definition of pastoral care can be proffered: Pastoral care is the communication of the gospel verbally, dynamically, and symbolically in interpersonal relationships that refer, however implicitly, to the community of faith. The verbal dimension of communication refers to what the minister says, for example, a word of forgiveness in response to a confession. The dynamic dimension refers to the energy components of communication, including the relation of the verbal to the nonverbal signs (e.g., are they congruent?). The dynamics of communication have much to do with the energy levels that characterize the interpersonal relationship, especially the conflict of energy, and thus include topics such as resistance. My understanding of communication includes the qualities of interpersonal interaction as a vital aspect of the communication. In other words, while the content of the message is integral, the message is embodied as well in the manner of its presentation. Christ in us ministers in what we say and in how we act. The symbolic dimension of communication underlines the fact that some of our words and actions take on meanings that far exceed their obvious import or the intentions we bring to them. The fact that the pastor phones a parishioner who has just returned home from the hospital has a symbolic meaning in that the ordained individual represents the ministry and care of the whole people of God.

A metaphoric understanding of Word generates a surfeit of meaning, to use Ricoeur's phrase, that yields an understanding of pastoral care much broader than a "preaching" model of pastoral care (e.g., that of Eduard Thurneysen) and yet locates pastoral care in the context of the entire ministry of the church and the role of the ordained ministry. Of course, this particular metaphor has been vital to the Protestant tradition, even though that tradition's understanding of the Word has been applied in narrow, unimaginative ways to the realities of the church's ministry. At the same time, it is apparent from renewal of biblical studies in the Roman Catholic Church and from numerous forms of renewal in its organization and missional life, that appreciation and understanding of the Word as root metaphor of Christian faith is growing. I shall say more shortly about how this metaphor relates to developments in the pastoral field. For now I state my belief that ministry of the Word, understood as a root metaphor, promises to help pastors envision the meaning of pastoral care for our time. It places self-understanding of ministry in a different framework from that of the healing of disease, where discontinuity is emphasized. (One can compare the psychoanalytic or other illness models of pastoral care and note that conflict and illness models have a certain affinity with each other.) Likewise, the metaphor of the Word places pastoral care in a different context from the one implied by the organismic metaphor that undergirds the eductive and educative approaches of much of the humanistic psychology found in the ministry of the church. The organismic model ingeniously envisions the importance and vitality of continuity in human affairs. The Word both unifies and breaks apart. The communication and sense of community it articulates are virtually structured by a dialectic of continuity and discontinuity. As a voice of forgiveness, judgment, or guidance, the Word encompasses various moments in the life of God's people. Accordingly, this basic metaphor encourages the kind of rich balance and blend of numerous metaphors that Don Browning suggests are essential to practical moral thinking.[5]

One can compare this contrasting versatility of the Word as source of orientation, disorientation, and reorientation with Donald Capps's emphasis on the orienting role of pastoral care.[6] Relying on Erik Erikson, Capps looks to the ratio between positive and negative poles in the developmental process that progresses in a series of bipolar stages. The hope is that the positive can outweigh the negative with the consequence that the negative adds depth and complexity to healthy growth. Given the two-edged character of the Word, the ministry of the Word model notes that serving our own good can either create wholeness or disrupt our own constructions for the sake of a more profound and abiding reorientation.

COMMUNICATION AND COMMUNITY

The ministry of the Word is a model that highlights the role of communication. The pastor is a communicator in all phases of his or her work. Whether verbally or nonverbally, when the pastor communicates the pastor ministers. Precisely because this model sees the essence of ministry as communication, it attributes great importance to community. Communication is the formation of community through meaningful actions. Sociologist Charles H. Cooley claimed that communication is "the mechanism through which relations exist and develop."[7]

The church as the institutional representation of the community of faith looks to the Word as its foundation. In Christ is its life, and its task is to communicate the gospel given by and embodied in Christ. Thus it calls people to faith despite the alienation that inevitably and persistently arises in our lives. The church calls us to faith in worship and witness. When communication is understood in a fundamental way with the Word as the core image, the life, worship, and witness of the church entail the verbal announcement of God's transcendent deeds and extend to symbolic actions. For this reason, to consider the church's ministry as communication of the Word is not to relegate sacraments to a secondary status but to understand them as actions that communicate the gospel. Nor is service an aftermath of verbal proclamation, as if action flowed naturally from conscious understanding. Love of neighbor and social service are meaningful actions that lure us to faith despite our human brokenness, and to participation in the community of faith.

If ministry of the Word can be understood so as to give due regard to the sacramental and social aspects of the church's task, can these dimensions be reinterpreted in relation to the concept of communication? Without the corrective of viewing ministry as communication, sacramental ministry may devolve into magic. That God communicates in the grace of the sacraments indicates that genuine disclosure as well as enactment take place. Though the meaning of God's disclosure in Christ is never exhausted, the sacraments impart grace in a way that is not arbitrary or mechanical. Sacramental theology requires the concept of ministry as communication. Likewise, without the perspective that ministry as communication provides, Christian service degenerates into busyness, whether managerial, political, or personal. The church and its leadership have the responsibility to discern for a given time which actions carry symbolic weight, that is, give glory to God.

The term "communication" derives from the Latin *communicatus,* to impart, participate, which in turn is formed from *communis,* meaning common. The latter term comes from *munus,* which means service or gift.[8] The basic concept suggested is the sharing of ideas, perspectives, and experiences, so that these are held in common. The etymology further suggests that this process of communication is a service or entails the giving and receiving of gifts. Perhaps the model of ministry as communication is not so separate as is frequently supposed from the notion of ministry as service.

Accordingly, for the sake of order, the church appoints ordained ministers of the Word. These persons are appointed leaders in the church's mission of communicating the gospel. They lead in teaching the Word, communicating the substance of the love of God in Christ to the church and world. They lead in setting an example in word and deed of communicating the gospel, and thereby induce and challenge professing Christians to be faithful to their ministry. Finally, ordained ministers symbolize the ministry of all Christians. This study examines the implications of such an understanding for the place of empathy and confrontation in pastoral care.

COMMUNITY AND CHARACTER

Since the subject is the implications of ministry of the Word for pastoral care, the relationship of the community and the individual is of vital importance. Indeed, this relationship is the central context for pastoral care as ministry of the Word in interpersonal relationships. Of course, the topic is both broad and complex, so I do not presume to deal with it exhaustively. The task of the community at both social and political levels in relation to the individual is not to maximize the latitude for people to do whatever they want so long as what they do does not deny others a comparable latitude. Rather, the task is to maximize opportunities for persons to develop their sense of moral worth. Thus, the mission of the institutional church so far as individuals are concerned is to nurture the formation of character that is rooted spiritually and morally in the image of Christ. When the church is faithful to this calling, it can be a vehicle of divine grace for the good of the person. One task of the church, then, is to manifest the grace of God in Christ as the basis of social respect and self-esteem. This understanding eschews self-righteousness, which presumes that human action and self-affirmation are independent of divine grace. At the same time it recognizes that grace has consequences for the human spirit and character.

I proffer this understanding of community and character as a corrective to modern individualism. Our culture is emerging from the "Me Decade" and does not yet have perspective on the ideology of intimacy that persists.[9] It is time to question concern for the welfare of the individual at the expense of the welfare of the community in modern, liberal societies. For the most part, modern pastoral care sets aside or puts temporarily in brackets the standards of the institutional church as representative of the community of faith, in order to attend to the needs of the indi-

vidual. Surely, the rights and needs of the person are vital, nor
can one assume that the health of the individual and the church
community coincide in every situation. Even so, ultimately the
welfare of the individual and the welfare of the community are
correlative concerns and must be treated as such. Living in a time
when the therapeutic orientation questions public commit-
ments[10] and when narcissistic character disorders increase, we
require a positive vision of the essential role of communication
and community in the life of the individual. An understanding of
the good of the person that does not articulate the constructive
(affirmative) role of community is unrealistic in that it artificially
separates the life of the individual from social reality.

A community is composed of the ways persons relate to and
communicate with one another. These ways persist in structures,
ideas, and rules that virtually give birth to the individual and
nurture the person. At the same time the community comes to
stand in relation to the individual so that one can address issues
about the relation of the individual to the community and vice
versa. The importance of community and the way in which the
welfare of the individual is tied to the community are conspicuous
themes in Scripture. It is God's people who are being saved, not
merely the lone individual. In the pastoral care field, Harry
DeWire articulates the importance of community and communication. He does this by understanding communication as an inner
dialogue that is extended through communication to others, and
that by virtue of this extension becomes personal commitment to
others. He goes on to say, "The goal of this commitment in the
Christian context is to maintain and develop a community of
thought and action based upon the will and work of God's
spirit."[11] Though he is right in the direction he takes and insight-
ful in the connection he draws between communication and
commitment, DeWire errs in starting with the individual rather
than the community. Understanding commitment as a consequence of inner dialogue once it is extended to others in communication, he assumes the inner dialogue is primal. But the
social psychologist and philosopher George Herbert Mead has
shown how this inner dialogue or the sociality of the self arises out

of interpersonal contact.[12] The first significance of an emphasis on communication is an appreciation of the role of the community in the drama of salvation.

To explore the relation of the community and the individual further, consider the person as a communication system. The formation of a social self wherein consciousness is a communication between self as subject (immediate awareness) and self as object constitutes a communication system wherein a person talks to self just as to another person. A surface reading of social self theory may lead one to think that if the self is a social creation, then society may change the self at will.[13] Indeed, other persons and society as a whole influence the individual at many levels. Nevertheless, the fact that the person forms a society within by maintaining an inner dialogue that is not totally exposed to outside reality provides for a measure of self-determination and for the possibility of transcending one's cultural values. Consequently, while social self theory emphasizes the role of community in individual development, it also accounts for autonomy and creative participation of persons in their cultures. This point is critical, since pastoral ministry has on the one hand the task of strengthening the person's participation in the community whenever feasible, and on the other hand the task of caring about the person even under tragic conditions wherein a conflict exists between the good of the individual and the good of the community.

Because of the possibility of an irreducible integrity, the person may transcend the community. Furthermore, healthy communities adapt to the creative influences of individuals. At the same time community transcends individuals, for when personal contributions are appropriated through social channels, personal intentions and meanings frequently are transformed according to the needs of the time and situation. In the midst of the tension between individual and society, either pole of social reality claims absolute dominance over the other out of a fear of the other's power to transcend. Contrariwise, the community trusts in and relies on the individual, and the individual risks trust in a commitment to the community on the basis of a primordial faith in a reality that transcends both, relativizing both yet working through both and thoroughly in both. God is the center of social and personal realities.

Having acknowledged my concern about individualism and my intent to underscore the essential sociality assumed in a communication model of ministry, I gladly concede that this direction has its risks. Whether institutional, sectarian or tribal, a vision of community can degenerate into idolatry. God is the generating and ultimate partner in any social vision of reality. The independent, inner dialogue of the person abstracted from relationship to God can be exaggerated into an idolatrous autonomy. Unchallenged by a call to reach out to the stranger, interpersonal intimacy becomes an all too familiar form of idolatry. Unchecked by the classics of a tradition and the creative insights of its individual members, a community readily exalts the status quo beyond any reasonable measure of justice or mercy. I hope it is clear that to emphasize the importance of community in the life of the individual is not to advocate the dominance of community in any of its forms over the individual.

When the above reflection is narrowed from community in its many senses to the concept of community of faith, the moral dimension of the relation of community and personhood becomes evident. Community forms character and character reforms community. At first I noted that a communication model of ministry gives emphasis to community. Now I observe that this model highlights character formation as well. As an example, note how personal growth often proceeds through the selection of character models and the subsequent absorption of the orientation and behavior of these model persons for one's own development. In Christian perspective, the community of faith is the body of Christ (Eph. 1:23; 4:16), and Christ is being formed in each member of the community. The process of communication is a process of moral and spiritual transformation. In fact, from a theological viewpoint, Christ is the one true minister. Our ministry is a participation in his ministry, a participation through communication of his name and spirit. How appropriate, then, that the Clinical Pastoral Education movement has centered on the personhood of the minister. What matters so often is one's availability as a person to others. I believe that the question of personal availability is a matter of character formation through a relational, communicative, learning process—that is, through participation in community.

In short, the motif of communication discloses the centrality of character formation through participation in community. For all the benefits of insight into the social, spiritual, and moral aspects of this vision of ministry, we dare not close the circle here. Otherwise, the vision remains general and promises to be only visionary. As a learning process, character formation involves more than the development of commitment. It entails the development of competencies and skills.

CHARACTER AND COMMUNICATION SKILLS

The task, then, is to elaborate the meaning of character formation as a learning process advanced through communication. Indeed, the challenge is to articulate the meaning of character in a manner that clarifies what is involved in detail. This undertaking is essential to the requirement that ministers be able to specify their areas of competence and responsibility. Such a requirement currently has introduced a tension in the Clinical Pastoral Education movement. We may hope that this will turn out to be a creative tension. Clinical Pastoral Education supervisors stand in a tradition that places confidence in learning as a doing/reflecting process that is highly intuitive. Furthermore, many are suspicious of theoretical or behavioral accounts of the learning process that appear to reduce it to a formula that virtually eliminates uncertainty and risk. On the other hand, the Clinical Pastoral Education movement is being called on to give an account of what is and is not being learned by participation in Clinical Pastoral Education. Supervisors face the challenge to be specific in rendering accounts of their ministry without abandoning the value of a holistic emphasis on the person. I hope that a concept of character formation that necessarily entails skills development without being reducible to the acquisition of specifiable operations will be suggestive to both the Clinical Pastoral Education movement and to parish pastors who look for resources to increase accountability in the context of ministry as both a calling and a profession.

While there is no formula for character development, the concept entails the notion of habit. Speaking of virtues, Aristotle noted that they are "implanted in us neither by nature nor contrary to nature: we are by nature equipped with the ability to receive them, and habit brings this ability to completion and fulfillment."[14] I shall follow this path in the elaboration of what character entails. Probably the reader is familiar with the description of stages of development in the human life cycle, especially Kohlberg's moral stages, James Fowler's stages of faith, and Erik Erikson's schedule of characterological virtues.[15] Such theories may help identify the formal nature of such development. I intend to study how development proceeds, regardless of stage, in relation to communication. The concept of habit is vital here, for character is the nurturing of God's gifts through habit, with the result that these gifts become integrated into personality as a "second nature."

Much of the habit that contributes to character is engaged through the influence of model persons on our lives. The learning can be further advanced and consolidated through a structured educational process that is designed to develop communication skills. For my purposes it is important that communication skills be added to the idea of character and that communication skills be understood in the moral and spiritual contexts of character development. With this in mind, especially for the task of elaborating the concrete meaning of empathy and confrontation, I shall make use of the emerging research in counseling psychology that analyzes such skills. In the course of applying this literature, however, I intend to reinterpret the significance of these skills. Typically they are presented in the pragmatic context of effectively influencing others. I understand communication skills training to be a form of moral education. For pastoral ministry, skills are understood in the context of character, community of faith, and communication of the gospel.

Accordingly, skills are symbols in which the Word is compressed and represented.

EMPATHY AND CONFRONTATION

The literature on communication skills in counseling psychology is vast, and various formats organize the data. The structure set forward in this study is based on the heuristic question concerning the relation of empathy to confrontation. I analyze communications skills in terms of an empathy cluster of skills and a confrontation cluster of skills. In this way the larger picture of the meanings of empathy and confrontation will be preserved as a detailed account of the behavioral manifestations of empathy and confrontation is developed. The key to how empathy and confrontation are related derives from the theological model of ministry and its moral implications, not from a micro-skills level of analysis. The behavioral analysis spells out how the gospel is conveyed in pastoral conversation with individuals and confirms the thesis about how empathy and confrontation are related.

Several questions contribute to the formation of the empathy and confrontation clusters of skills to be introduced in chapters 3 and 4: Is the behavior teachable in the sense that it occurs in ordinary settings and can be further developed in structured exercises? Does the behavior represent an area of practical interest among pastors? Is the communication behavior amenable to theological interpretation; that is, can it be understood as a concrete expression of ministry of the Word? Can the behavior be exhibited readily in a one-to-one conversation? On the basis of such questions the empathy cluster of skills consists of empathy proper, physical attending, concreteness, genuineness; and the confrontation cluster of skills consists of confrontation proper, self-disclosure, immediacy, and interpretation. These skills will be defined and discussed later, but let me explain immediately that interpretation here does not refer to psychological interpretations of persons' situations or behavior that are communicated to them in counseling. Most psychological counselors rely very little on such interpretation, but when they do interpret people's behavior and situations, they do so primarily from the perspective of their profession. Likewise, when interpretation is called for, pastors should rely on the resources of their profession— theological sources.

My thesis is that respect is the theological and moral value that relates empathy and confrontation as ways of communicating the gospel in pastoral care. The effectiveness of empathy in helping persons depends on its promise of communicating respect for persons, a respect or positive regard that is analogous to God's valuing of persons and that therefore may become the occasion for the person's discovering or "hearing" God's care and acceptance at a deeper level. Likewise, the effectiveness of confrontation in helping persons depends on how respectfully they are challenged. Even in psychological literature, guidelines for effective confrontation are for the most part guidelines for responsible confrontation. Effective confrontation is responsible insofar as it maintains and strengthens respect for the person. Consequently, empathy and confrontation are moments in the communication of caring respect. The concept of respect is the key that enables a meaningful exploration of the interplay of empathy and confrontation in pastoral ministry. This study tries to bring out the common meaning of empathy and confrontation in the framework of communicating the gospel and to examine in behavioral detail how empathy and confrontation are manifested in pastoral conversations. They are forms of communication essential both to participation in a community of faith and to the process of character formation.

The question of the relation of empathy and confrontation keeps this study to a manageable size at the cost of not analyzing the entire range of communication skills. I do not claim that the two clusters of skills examined here exhaust the behavioral manifestations of interpersonal communication. At the same time, the ground covered in this study is sufficiently varied that most pastors will find understanding and practical guidance for personal growth and for expanding their repertoire of caring responsiveness to persons.

For purposes of convenience and economy, I have limited the discussion to one-to-one conversations. Though much of the material presented in this study readily applies to group work and family ministry, this application is not pursued. One should not infer that group dynamics and family systems are phenomena that can be reduced to interpersonal skills.

Though this project includes a general theological account of empathy and confrontation in relation to communicating the gospel, to the community of faith, and to character development, one will not find herein a complete guide to reflection on one's pastoral work from a theological perspective. When examining an act of ministry as recorded in notes, a case conference report, or a verbatim, one needs to use theological resources in ways that go beyond the assessment of communication skills. Though the discussion will be limited, the analysis of interpretation as a communication skill will provide clues to the use of theological resources in the pastoral interpretation of what people present to their ministers.

This chapter has introduced the idea of ministry of the Word for purposes of examining the relation of empathy and confrontation. The following chapter will examine in more detail the model of communication that is the basis for the thesis about empathy and confrontation. This model emerges from the basic concept of the Word as root metaphor of ministry.

CHAPTER 2

Principles of Communication in Pastoral Care

A review of pastoral care literature suggests that the theories of communication in pastoral care have been in search of a root metaphor that is adequate to the pastoral task. I shall argue that limitations in previous theories of communication in pastoral care most often reflect limitations in understanding the Word as a multifaceted metaphor. After this interpretation, the chapter enumerates principles of communication that give direction to the practical discussion that ensues in the remainder of the book.

THEORIES IN SEARCH OF A METAPHOR

No professional movement[1] comes to fulfillment without a reigning metaphor that guides theory and practice. Academic and practical debates in a field of inquiry typically give expression to various metaphors that compete for ascendance. Even so, intellectual and professional movements are not always self-conscious about these phenomena and consequently may not make full use of the metaphor or metaphors available in principle to them. This is the situation, I believe, with the modern pastoral care movement. While dominant in academic psychology, behaviorism and behavioral psychologies were virtually anathema in the rise of pastoral care and pastoral theory. But especially within the last decade, an expanding diversity has come to mark the field. Now numerous books advise pastors about the use of behavioral techniques and examine behavioral explanation from a theological perspective.[2] Meanwhile, the psychoanalytic tradition continues as a vital force in the pastoral field because of its integration of depth dimensions with technological reason and its sense of the tragic limits of life. Pastoral psychology's initial encounters with Gordon Allport and Carl Rogers have blossomed into an extensive literature on growth therapies, personal fulfillment, and small groups. It seems that pastoral care as a professional discipline is moving everywhere at once, and so the generalists in the parish have little sense of where leaders in this field might take them. The eclectic approach in Howard Clinebell's *Basic Types of Pastoral Counseling* in 1966[3] is the precursor of this trend. Some fear that this diversity is symptomatic of rootless confusion. Others rejoice that reigning orthodoxies have been cast down in favor of freer thought and practice. In my own view the diversity does have the freshness of new inquiry, yet this is a transitional time that will pass. As metaphor, ministry of the Word has the capacity to help us build on the strengths inherent in the pastoral care movement's development and to adumbrate ways in which the present diversity in pastoral care can be shaped toward an integrated vision. The concept of communication to which the metaphor is tied is at home in both religious and secular worlds. How have the metaphor and the concept been treated in modern pastoral care literature? And how can analysis of the metaphor inform principles that clarify the concept of communication and guide its application?

Care as Proclamation

One cannot think of the language of communication or proclamation in pastoral care without recalling Eduard Thurneysen's *Theology of Pastoral Care.*[4] This Barthian theologian defines pastoral care as proclaming the Word to the individual. His analysis does not imply that no dialogue takes place. Actually, Thurneysen allows that the pastor should listen carefully and caringly to the person's concerns before any proclamation of the gospel. Furthermore, he is sensitive to the fact that the pastor hears the Word in pastoral conversations as well as does the parishioner. Astutely, he also understands how the word of grace is resisted and he alerts his readers to expect such responses. In this way a

dynamic or conflictual factor, at least on the surface, is acknowledged. For all this, however, listening is for Thurneysen little
more than a preliminary exercise to the essential moment when
the pastor has something to say that is not his own wisdom but the
announcement of forgiveness. Unfortunately, Thurneysen offers only a few examples of pastoral letters to distressed persons.
The more significant shortcoming, however, relates to the
monological character of Thurneysen's model. That is, though
there are hints of the dialogical character of one-to-one encounters, a one-way model of communication seems forced onto an
essentially dialogical situation. Since such an imposition is not
supported by case study and verbatim demonstrations of its practical effectiveness, Thurneysen's approach has not been well re-
ceived, at least in America. The fault my own assessment finds in
Thurneysen lies in his not being aware of the metaphorical
character of proclamation of the Word. Had his vision been more
fundamental and broader, he would not have been so literal nor
concentrated so exclusively on verbal proclamation in the pastoral conversation. His understanding of the dynamics of interpersonal communication was limited to seeing a tendency in many to
resist the message of forgiveness, and he seems to have missed
entirely the symbolic character of action. Even so, since the verbal
level of communication has not been treated adequately in modern pastoral care, and in particular since the role of verbal interpretation of Christian faith has been neglected, Thurneysen's
contribution should not be summarily dismissed but can be the
occasion for a reconsideration of verbal communication of the
gospel. However briefly, John Cobb argues that pastors should
not shy away from verbal communication of the gospel in pastoral
conversations.[5] Likewise, Donald Capps argues that proclamation of the gospel can be more nuanced than directive approaches
realize and offers a model of indirective counseling, related to
parabolic communication, as an example.[6] It should be noted,
however, that Jay Adams's concept of nouthetic counseling rein-
troduces a verbal proclamation model that is more literalistic than
is Thurneysen's, that is overly directive, and that is insensitive to

the dynamic and symbolic dimensions of communication in pastoral care.[7] Approaches to pastoral conversations that emphasize how the gospel is proclaimed nonverbally in pastoral care are often used by pastors and pastoral counselors who offer more psychological interpretation to persons than they do theological interpretation. These approaches fall short of setting forth a balanced view of pastoral care that provides guidance at both verbal and nonverbal levels.

Care as Dialogue

Published two years after the appearance in English of Thurneysen's ponderous approach to pastoral care as proclamation, Reuel Howe's *The Miracle of Dialogue* introduces a note of grace in its unpretentious and articulate reflection on human communication. Inspired by Martin Buber's *I and Thou*,[8] Howe saw the principle of dialogue—openness to the other side—as the basis of communication. Given the sufficiency and moral worth of the principle of dialogue, any monologue—unless it be diverted cleverly to the service of the principle of dialogue—signaled lack of communication. The moralistic valuation of monologue counters Thurneysen's understanding of communication as proclamation and proffers in its place an inspired, if somewhat idealistic, account of dialogue in which persons are called to be open to others, that is, experience the other person from that one's own perspective. Howe rightly applies the principle of dialogue in many arenas, from informal interpersonal encounters to politics, but no audience has responded more warmly than has American pastoral care. Suddenly, dialogue became a perspective for interpretation of the doctrines of creation and redemption, since the miracle of dialogue, according to Howe, is that "it can bring relationship into being, and it can bring into being once again a relationship that has died."[9] This sensible appeal to openness, at once a religious and romantic value, advances the humanistic spirit in pastoral care. Of course, Howe wins the debate, if that is its character, against Thurneysen—but not without cost. At any rate, it seems to me that the transcendent flows too easily from Howe's account of dialogue, for here transcendence is simply immanence with a capital "I." How does one stop short of idolatry or over-evaluation of the other side? How does one gain critical perspective on inspirational encounters with other people? Suppose that human experience is not solely grounded in an alternating dialectic of pragmatic relationships and intuitively elevated personal encounters, but is also founded on, and formed out of, fundamental metaphors that disclose our situation? Such metaphors have an objectivity in relation to subjective experience. They organize, energize, and direct experience. They make us what we are, individually and as a community, and they enable us to dream what we can be. Beyond an intuitively persuasive account of the possibilities of the present moment, the meaning of dialogue is founded on a primordial hearing of the Other who has become the Same in Jesus Christ, and consequently on memory, a listening to narrative as the prose of our becoming, and on hope as attending to metaphor, the poetry of our being. Metaphor and story give birth to dialogue. By the Word we are called, claimed, set aside, and trusted to participate in dialogue. Dialogue is not primarily a matter of miraculous immediacy in the present moment, but occurs on the basis of a primordial reference to the past and the future embodied in Jesus Christ. In other words, there is no dialogue on human terms—no dialogue *ex nihilo*.

What is lacking in Howe's classic study is addressed in a fine book by Heije Faber and Ebel van der Schoot, *The Art of Pastoral Conversation*. Their approach appropriates wholeheartedly what can be learned from the client-centered, nondirective approach to counseling. Accordingly, for them the pastoral conversation is a dialogue in which the feelings of the person with whom a pastor converses are to be explored caringly and empathically. Out of sensitivity to the induction principle, they recognize yet advocate great caution with regard to elements in conversation such as suggestion, persuasion, and interpretation. Even so, the final aim of pastoral conversation is "to help the other person see his life in God's light."[10] Furthermore, the pastor does not enter into the conversation on his own authority, but rather, as one who is commissioned and charged by God, he or she endeavors to assist the person to understand that Christ is present in all circumstances, especially the ones shared in conversation with the pastor. The pastor tries to help the person to see all of experience in God's light. Influenced by the experience-centered perspective and the clinical method of American pastoral care, on the one hand, and by the Barthian approach of Europe, on the other, these authors try to describe a dialogue that discovers the presence of a Third Party, or a conversation that prepares for a proclamation of the Word. The authors acknowledge that ". . . the switch over from pastoral in the general sense to pastoral in its specialized sense, from reflecting to preaching the gospel, has several aspects which can only be brought into relief by more empirical study and deeper thinking about principles. . . ."[11] Indeed, though sprinkled generously throughout with helpful case examples of pastoral conversations, the link between the person-centered dialogue and proclamation of the Word in an interpersonal situation is held up as an ideal and as a bald empirical fact hallowed by not a little mystery.

This approach corrects Thurneysen's de-emphasis on listening in favor of the event of proclamation. It also corrects the contrary tendency to de-emphasize verbal proclamation in favor of the implicit communication of grace by way of interpersonal dynamics. Still, the Faber and van der Schoot model retains a pattern like Thurneysen's: listening first as preparation, followed by the distinctively pastoral moment when the Word is recapitulated in the words of the conversation. Furthermore, though it is not clear from reading *The Art of Pastoral Conversation*, I believe it is faithful to the authors' intent and vision to suggest that the evangelical Word precedes the pastoral relationship and establishes the possibility of pastoral conversation (as its Alpha) and directs the aim and fulfillment of the pastoral conversation (as its Omega). I do not promise that my approach will resolve all the mystery to which *The Art of Pastoral Conversation* refers, as if any approach could, but I do hope to advance our understanding beyond the comment, "I would just like to say that it must leave a great deal to intuition grounded on the right attitude toward both the patient and ourselves."[12]

Care as Interpersonal

The interpersonal perspective articulated by Paul Johnson gives expression to some of the themes developed here. His concept of responsive counseling appreciates the values of non-directive counseling yet suggests that there is greater variety in the ways pastors can be responsive to what persons bring to them. While aware of the limits of directive approaches, Johnson envisions a pastoral relationship that does not overvalue the subjective perspectives of the individual but operates out of hope in the mutual interactions of persons. Given this relational emphasis, Johnson rightly stresses the centrality of communication in pastoral care and suggests the significance of community for pastoral ministry. In his view ultimate reality has a relational character.[13] My own study attempts to build on this and similar works by placing the interpersonal perspective in the context of ministry of the Word, examining in greater detail some elements of communication, and reinterpreting their significance in light of the communication model and the ministry of the Word.

Dialogical understanding of pastoral care may be grounded in humanistic or existential traditions. The I-Thou approach to dialogue as advanced by Buber and Howe relies on both, but the existentialist perspective on the irrational, tragedy and alienation merits additional discussion. Generally this approach to ministry is less optimistic than the above dialogical approach in that the alienation of the person from self and society is so great that no flowering of individuals into genuine community is made possible simply by removing barriers to communication. For the existentialist, ministry has its focus on the meaninglessness of life to the individual in a depersonalized situation. Ministry is a confrontation of the individual to help the person discover meaning and consequently be reconciled with the human condition in a personal way. It was Victor Frankl who first introduced questions of existential frustration and modern meaninglessness to many pastors.[14] From a different perspective Carl Jung also raises this issue.[15] With the existentialist's stance came a strong emphasis on individual responsibility. In radical versions, responsibility means that one creates one's own meaning out of nothing. Though appreciation for communal tradition is acknowledged by the likes of Martin Heidegger, the locus of meaning resides within the person for most existentialists. In the early existentialism of Berdayev, for example, the individual houses a pristine self within. On the whole the existential spirit in pastoral care has not served to uproot the extensive individualism of the West. The ministry of the Word metaphor requires a relational perspective.

THESES REGARDING COMMUNICATION IN PASTORAL CARE

The relationship between fundamental vision or root metaphor, conceptual theory, and practical guidelines is not a simple relationship in which one vision implies, in all situations, one theory of communication, which in turn can be elaborated in a set of guidelines. Accordingly, I do not claim that the following is a complete theory of communication in pastoral care or that it is the only way to elaborate the Word as metaphor. The principles introduced here, however, do identify significant conceptual links between the Word as metaphor and elements of interpersonal communication as skills that can be taught. The following theses help to relate the thrust of the metaphoric vision of ministry of the Word and the practical discussion of the relation of empathy and confrontation in pastoral conversations.[16]

Communication Discloses

From a theological viewpoint the ultimate hope of communication is that the divine-human relation be disclosed. The process of discovery of what had been hidden or at least not fully understood characterizes communication, whether the vehicles of disclosure be the content of words, the dynamics of interpersonal relations, or acts of human behavior.

One implication of this thesis is that human behavior communicates when it discloses our relation with God. Sigmund

Freud undertook to demonstrate the continuity of communication and action, for he explored the implications of the idea that
all actions are meaningful. Consequently, inadvertent slips of the
tongue or seemingly senseless behaviors were, for him, in principle interpretable, for they disclosed meaning in the very attempt
to conceal. Freud did not relate the meaning of actions to the
divine-human relation, but he did discuss their meaning in terms
of intra-psychic conflicts. By way of comparison, behaviorists
attribute a kind of meaning to behavior in terms of the conditions
and consequences of behavior. Despite their emphasis on behavior, they sell short its significance because they do not have a way
to envision the symbolic significance of behavior. Watzlawick
correctly asserts that we cannot not communicate,[17] for properly
understood behavior communicates more than common sense
understands. Yet not all behavior discloses the divine-human
relation with identical force. So while in principle all behavior
may be interpretable as disclosing something of the divine-
human story, it should be acknowledged that at particular times
certain behaviors have greater symbolic impact than others. Both
the universal potential of action to speak and the realistic limits in
particular situations are important considerations. Throughout
its history the church has believed that contemplation is a form of
action, yet a failure to appreciate the communicative power of the
behavioral has contributed to times when a quietistic emphasis on
contemplation has separated the world of contemplation from
the world of action. On the other side, because a missional or
liberation theology of action pays insufficient attention to the
possibilities of selective actions to disclose the divine presence and
promise in the midst of human oppression, its representatives at
times attend more to political strategy than to symbolic force. One
reason to connect pastoral care to the metaphor of the Word is
that action may express meaning and not be mere busyness or a
reduction to coping with problems. As T. S. Eliot wrote,

Teach us to care and not to care
Teach us to sit still.[18]

Between the solitary figure who meditates on life and the tragic hero who acts and, in acting, both bears the burdens of conflict and suffers is the One who is the Word. A disclosive model of communication embraces contraries and in so doing limns a wholeness that characterizes the mission of the church and the task of pastoral care.

In principle all action is interpretable or related to communication; select actions under particular circumstances communicate with especially powerful, symbolic force. Likewise, in principle all words induce action; select words provoke action and evoke relationship. Consequently, not mere speech, wordiness, or thoughts clothing themselves however elegantly in words constitute communication. When inaugurated through words, communication par excellence leads to meaningful action.

Finally, communication discloses the presence of God in relation to both our best and our worst attitudes and behavior. However inadequate in light of past achievements, present needs, and future aspirations, our best efforts are not independent of the gracious power of God present in our lives, and we may hope that they are genuine expressions of gratitude for the grace of God at work in us. Courage to divulge, or at least face, our worst is made possible by the accepting and forgiving grace of God in us. Communication that discloses dimensions of the divine-human relation inevitably encompasses such contrasts, exposing us to multiple meanings of God's grace.[19]

As disclosive communication, ordained ministry has its foundation, model, and reality in Jesus Christ as the Word of God, the Revealer of God. The ministry of the Word is his ministry, and we share in it (John 1:1, 14).

Communication Is Process

Communication transcends the singular event and its circumstances. Communication is a process whereby individuality and community are formed. What is the nature of communication as disclosure? Two powerful answers to this question merit consideration. The first answer claims that disclosure is event. According to this view, truth comes to us in an I-Thou relation which is immediate and momentary. It arises out of the ordinary, everyday event. It transforms the event in that a genuine Thou encounters us, creating the I that corresponds to the Thou, the I that is connected in solidarity with the universe in a personal way. In this vision of the reality of disclosure, life is baptized with miraculous occasions that, however occasional or fleeting, renew our sense of belonging to life and show us the eternal in the present I-Thou relation.[20] The second answer sees disclosure as a process, however harmonious or conflicted, whereby one participates in community, contributing to the solidarity and creativity of a larger enterprise, and being formed oneself over a lifetime into the likeness of the One who calls. Though the first answer allows that past encounters may be bound up again in a new event, a process approach emphasizes how events and relationships cumulatively influence personal development over time. The first answer stresses the qualitative gap between the process of individuation and the moment of personal encounter, since the former is built on separation and the latter is a matter of connectedness. The second answer believes that an element of continuity links pragmatic strategies with an underlying personal, communal quality that is present in the total flow of life. In the disclosure interpreted according to the event paradigm, the event has a hallowed, set-aside quality, for the I-Thou relation is not conditioned by external variables. In the disclosure interpreted according to the process paradigm, events flow together in a process of personal becoming. Consequently, the significance of our decisions is not limited to how they impact immediate actions but includes how they shape our personal development and participation in community.[21]

The focus of much theological education with regard to pastoral care is the singular act of ministry as recorded in a verbatim report. This device is especially helpful for examining disclosure as event. The verbatim conference in Clinical Pastoral Education is often able to give attention to the immediate qualities of the relationship between minister and parishioner or between chaplain and patient. All too frequently, however, students and ministers in training seem at a loss when it comes to explicating human behavior in terms of moral principles and spiritual vision. In the verbatim report each event is an occasion that manifests the meaning of ministry, grace, brokenness, and the like. Though it is possible to examine developmental and characterological issues in the verbatim report, the situational focus means that one must make heroic leaps of the imagination from the bits and pieces of a singular event as recalled and reconstructed by the minister. In typical verbatim seminars spiritual formation and moral character make cameo appearances. Case studies lessen this difficulty by extending the reference beyond one event, but they do not assure attention to skills in the context of character development or spiritual formation. When one combines the limits of the verbatim report with the short-term nature of pastoral contacts in the institutional settings that make up the vast majority of Clinical Pastoral Education centers, it is no surprise that disclosure as event often dominates disclosure as process. Of course, there is much discussion of education as a process in Clinical Pastoral Education. How fitting it is to place equal emphasis on ministry as an ongoing process in which spiritual vision, character, and competence are being shaped.

According to the paradigm of disclosure as event, habit is an enemy of immediacy. By habit our expectations are present, making distortion of phenomena highly likely. In this way the person enters an event closed to the vast possibilities inherent in it. Usually the emerging of an I-Thou relation either entails the setting aside of the accumulations of habit or transcends the conditions surrounding the event. In the process paradigm, habit is not avoidable and furthermore can be helpful. Process relies on a measure of continuity between community and personal structures, the nurturing constancy of community and characterological reliability. To be sure, strong character is adaptable and flexible, not rigid. In addition, the formation of character is not reducible to learning by habit. Even so, habit contributes positively to the capacity of the individual to participate creatively in the ongoing life of the community. For the disclosure-as-process approach the conditioned quality of events and character is good news.

Communication Is Conditioned

To understand ministry of the Word as communication is to acknowledge that such ministry is conditioned culturally, interpersonally, and technologically. That is, ministry is not lifted up into some pure realm that is unaffected by human and empirical limitations. Hence, a theory of ministry attends both to purpose and to procedure. If a theory of ministry attends only to method, then a basic sense of direction may be lost. If an approach to ministry as communication elaborates only the generalities of direction and process, it fails to provide ministers with reference points for practical accountability. In relation to the inevitable conditioning that characterizes communication in ministry one should note two dangers: the first, that ministers become so enamored with the techniques and methods of communicating that they forget the goal; and the second, that ministers be so inspired by their vision of ministry as communication of the gospel that they assume that effective methods flow naturally from their grasp of basic principles. The former problem I call professionalism, the latter romanticism. Because it is enamored with techniques of communication, modern professionalism misses the essence of communication. Procedures change more rapidly than do theories of meaning but the more procedures change the more they stay the same. A change in meaning, however, can reorganize and redirect procedures. To compensate for the problems of professionalism, ministers may eschew method. Trusting totally in spontaneity, they run the risk of settling for the appearance of communication without the reality of it. The purpose of ministry cannot be reduced to the methods it may employ, yet its vision needs to be represented in particular methods that serve as symbols of basic intention. Without such concreteness, a theory of ministry never touches the ground of a pastor's daily work. The ordained ministry is both calling and profession, both gift and task.

One consequence of this understanding of ministry as conditioned communication is that in order to enhance communication one must practice in a disciplined fashion. Ministers' commitment to their calling ought to include a place for what John Dewey called "deliberate rehearsal."[22]

This is no less true for pastors' interpersonal communication than for their preaching and leading in corporate worship. A skills development component in pastoral education assumes an "already" and a "not yet" of grace and character.

Communication Is Dialogical Interpretation

Ministry is a process of communication among two or more persons who before God are equal in status. Consequently, ministry is dialogue between these persons. At the same time, one partner in this dialogue represents symbolically the Word communicating with people. In this capacity the ordained minister is assumed to be a consultant who brings to the conversation a resourcefulness in interpreting Scripture and the Christian tradition. In this respect the partners in a conversation are not equal, or at least the situation suggests that the minister has a particular responsibility as one who is trained to interpret. Such a description does not imply that ministers perform their function only when they explain and apply the meaning of Scripture to a personal situation. Rather, the relationship proceeds on the basis of a potential complementarity structured into the situation from the beginning.

This means that ministers engage in pastoral care with a certain authority and responsibility. They have been given authority to proclaim the Word and administer the sacraments. They do not forsake this authority when they enter the realm of personal celebrations and concerns. Of course this authority is to be actualized in accord with Christian teaching: ". . . whoever would be great among you must be your servant" (Matthew 20:26b). Therefore, ministers do not parade their authority, nor are they highhanded. They do not aim at dominance but aspire to service. Nor do they, because of this authority, preach to individuals. Yet their role as representatives of biblical texts and a history of interpretation does shape their behavior and perspective in pastoral care.

The minister's role as interpreter is analogous to the task of someone who translates the messages of two persons who are in dialogue but speak different languages. The translator interprets each one's language to the other. Likewise, the task of the minister entails a kind of interpretation of the person's message to Another and the interpretation of God's message to persons. In other words, in pastoral care as a dialogue, the minister cannot interpret God's Word without also interpreting the person's perspective. This image assumes that a "gap" divides the human and the divine and that this distance can be bridged.[23] The first implication is that the minister must know the "language of the person," or as Hiltner has so well emphasized, must start where the person is.[24] For this reason, pastoral communication as dialogical interpretation requires that pastors be empathic and able to communicate their empathy to others.

As dialogue such conversations cannot be reduced to one perspective. While pastors have responsibility to help people clarify their own messages, they also are called to represent another perspective that may or not dovetail with what emerges from persons' self-expression. Though I do not know of any research among pastors or pastoral counselors of a similar nature, some research of psychotherapy notes that patients influence therapists more than therapists influence patients, in the sense that therapists adapt to clients more than vice versa. This may reflect the fact that therapists are more skilled interpersonally than their clients, but how do clients change if another is constantly adapting to them? Can therapists' openness to clients reinforce rather than transform past patterns of behavior? Though there is no simple answer to these questions, the issue for psychotherapists may be addressed to ministers. Can ministers be so adaptive to parishioners' expectations and perspectives that they encourage tendencies already within these persons to aggrandize themselves? To raise this question is to remind ministers that while we do owe understanding and empathy to people, we also represent a tradition that promises to speak to their hopes and needs. A genuine dialogue engages more than one perspective. Pastors have the opportunity to avoid pitting their own personal preferences against people's perspectives and to help people interpret their experiences and determine their responses in light of Christian understanding. Because more than one perspective is present in genuine dialogue, communication may involve confrontation. In principle, no confrontation that stands against a person's perspective can do so except for the sake of being for the person.

People move themselves to act by the descriptions they adopt of their world, selves, and God, as Hauerwas reminds us.[25] In dialogue people can clarify their own perspectives and submit them to the challenge of other interpretations. Ministers represent Christian understanding; they do not enjoy full comprehension. Thus, they are not authorized to impose their understanding on individuals, but can share their understanding in a manner that invites joint exploration.

Pastoral Communication Is Respectful Communication

Respect is the overriding moral consideration in pastoral care as communication of the gospel. In Jesus Christ, God has demonstrated how worthwhile he considers mankind and how immeasurably important is the value of the person. Our worth is grounded in God's respect disclosed in Jesus Christ, a respect not based on our goodness or achievements but on God's enduring desire to engage and enjoy us in wholesome relationship. When we show respect for one another we reflect this fundamental truth of our human condition: that despite our mortality, fallibility, and evil, God holds us in high esteem through Jesus Christ. To honor one another, furthermore, is a way in which we are called to return honor to God as our Creator and Redeemer. In this sense the moral life is an extension of our worship life. Morally, respect is an inherent dimension of pastoral ministry and therefore need not be justified on pragmatic grounds. Of course, relating to people with respect is likely to have good consequences, and psychologists can study such outcomes as much as they like. Still, respect is a moral imperative established primarily on our understanding of God's loving esteem given in Christ.

The remainder of the book is a practical commentary on empathy and confrontation as moral values in interpersonal communication that is grounded in respect. Given the controlling vision and the guiding theses on communication, the task now is to examine the relation of empathy and confrontation in some detail so that they can be understood as capacities that can be strengthened through practice and that are related integrally to each other on the basis of respect as a guiding moral principle.

With reference to ministry of the Word, the focus will be on the dynamic level of communicating the Word, not on the verbal or symbolic. This is appropriate for the study of the place of respect in relation to empathy and confrontation. The reader should understand, then, that what follows applies the model to a specific dimension of practice and is not a thorough exploration of the implications of the model for pastoral care.

CHAPTER 3

Listening and Empathy

The purpose of this chapter is to interpret the meaning of listening from the perspective of the previously discussed communication principles and a vision of the Word as metaphor. In this context the term "listening" is not to be taken literally. Rather the term functions here as itself a metaphor, representing a cluster of responses from pastors that help to educe parishioners' own perspectives, feelings, and experiences. The eductive goal assembles these responses around the core response, empathy. By reference to respect the discussion will highlight the moral significance of each of these responses or skills. Interpersonal respect is the human condition par excellence that promotes personal strength, responsibility, insight, and openness to others. Listening responses have power to educe because they impart large doses of accepting respect. In addition, listening nurtures a mutuality that enables persons to move beyond self-understanding or insight and interact constructively with others' confrontations, when those confrontations also are founded on respect. In other words, the respect that generates listening helps persons to listen to themselves and prepares them to listen to others and make wholesome use of others' perspectives and confrontations. Listening enacts participation in community on a limited basis and helps to ready persons for a broader participation in community characterized by enhanced mutuality. Guidelines with regard to listening skills are practical precisely to the extent that they are morally sensible. The point is not to listen because listening works. Rather, moral considerations give shape to listening, enhancing its effectiveness. This logic is the reverse of the pragmatism that dominates the current behavioral sciences. Accordingly, the approach here is to delineate theological and moral considerations in the direction of their practical consequences. Finally, portions of this chapter and the next address you, the reader, directly. They ask you to reflect in structured and imaginative ways on your own ministry. The intent is to facilitate immediate application of the principles and guidelines to your own situation. I hope you will be engaged by the suggested reflections and that they will help you to personalize the information acquired in these chapters.

The next chapter will discuss the place of respect in ministry as confrontational communication. At this point it is important to understand that the emphasis on respect in relation to listening means that ordinarily the respect communicated through empathy precedes respectful confrontation. Only in unusual circumstances can pastors confront respectfully without first listening respectfully. Indeed, empathy itself has a confrontational dimension in that empathic responses help persons to confront themselves. Viewed as a whole, competent pastoral communication goes beyond empathy. This means, however, that competent pastoral communication does not proceed by a different route to its goals but moves beyond empathy by building on the kind of listening that imparts respect and educes persons' own understanding of and responsibility for their problems and resources.

WHAT IS EMPATHY?

Let us begin to examine the core concept. What is empathy? According to *Webster's New Collegiate Dictionary*,[1] empathy is the capacity to participate in another's feelings or ideas. This definition can be compared with sympathy, which implies an identification with another's feelings or ideas. Empathy points to the gift, cultivated in various ways, for vicarious feeling with another. This vicarious experience depends on the capacity to project oneself imaginatively into another's experience. English and English go so far as to define empathy as the "apprehension of the state of mind of another person without feeling (as in *sympathy*) what the other feels."[2] Though this definition departs from popular usage, the major point is that empathy does not imply one's identification with another's feeling. One may understand another's rage, for example, but not necessarily identify with it. Empathy does refer to one's ability to take on another's viewpoint in the sense of adopting imaginatively and understandingly that person's own outlook. Better than any other concept empathy captures the idea of maintaining a kind of objectivity while at the same time participating in others' experience. In empathy one sets aside one's own viewpoint, or at least one's own response to what another describes and expresses, takes up the other person's way of seeing the universe or interpreting a situation, including feelings, and yet stops short of agreeing with the person, approving, disapproving, or identifying with the other's experience. Though one sets aside one's own viewpoint temporarily in empathy, one does not completely abandon that viewpoint. One envisions another's experience to understand it, not to make it one's own.

Empathy is both understanding and communicating that understanding to the person to whom one listens. When empathic pastors are aware of their own feelings in response to what they hear, they set these inner responses aside in order to project themselves imaginatively into the parishioner's message, and communicate their understanding to parishioners. The last step is essential, for empathy is a moral and relational skill, not simply a matter of inner comprehension of what another says. Ministry is communication, and empathy is a form of communication.

An elderly woman whose husband had died recently asked her pastor to visit her. During the visit she told him how one of her two stepsons had not accepted his father's revision of his will and believed that she was robbing him and his brother of much that was rightly theirs. She went on to tell the pastor how this stepson had beaten her before witnesses. She had consulted with a lawyer, she said, but she was still confused about what to do. In reflecting on the visit, the pastor reported, "Part of me wanted to go punch Joe in the nose for hitting a little old lady. But another part of me helped me keep my composure and I was able to deal with the situation professionally." At this point the pastor sorts out personal impulse and the need to respond caringly but objectively. The task of empathy is to put oneself imaginatively into this woman's place—without agreeing uncritically with her perspective, without making judgments of others based on her perceptions—and to communicate this understanding to her:

> Woman: "I've always loved both of those boys as if they were my own. I don't want to do the wrong thing. . . ."
> Pastor: "It's hard to make a decision when you've been hurt by someone you love."

Essentially, this pastor's response is empathic, though he would have done better to say, "It's hard to make a decision when you feel you've been hurt. . . ."

By being empathic ministers hope to establish or reaffirm a trusting quality in their relationships, help parishioners to clarify feelings, perceptions, and values, and stimulate exploration of parishioners' relationships with themselves, others, and God. Building trust often is helpful in itself, for trust undercuts the isolation that frequently brings persons to pastors. Empathy contributes to an experience of community at the level of interpersonal relationships with representatives of the church's ministry. In our coming to trust one another, personal bonds are formed that have their own value even when no change or cure seems possible. A person may be trusting simply because he or she is communicating with a minister. Or a pastor may have a long-standing relationship with a person in which trust clearly is present. Even so, empathy reaffirms and acknowledges the basis for that trust. Understanding responses are not to be neglected simply because trust is not an issue.

Furthermore, empathy serves a moral purpose by presenting persons with their own responsibility for their feelings, values, and perceptions. Empathy assists persons in that inner dialogue with themselves that promises to strengthen responsibility. By engaging persons in further exploration of their experiences, empathy communicates an expectation that they will assume responsibility for and accept their experiences as their own. To say that empathy serves these purposes is not to imply that conditions can be controlled in such a fashion that empathy always produces these outcomes.

BODILY ATTENDING

Communication does not start with words but with the body. Pastors who are alert to their own and others' bodily, nonverbal communication tend to learn to know others with facility and to develop personal relationships that are rich emotionally. Pastors who pay more attention to the content of what is said than to the nonverbal level of communication usually are more committed to solving problems than developing relationships. I believe that the expressive dimension of communication exceeds the practical dimension in value. While problem-solving is important, the management of problems is not the primary force energizing pastoral ministry.

In our culture, several nonverbal behaviors signal to people that they are receiving others' full attention. These behaviors include eye contact, open posture, a tendency to lean forward slightly, and the facing of persons squarely. When pastors exhibit these behaviors they communicate that they are attending fully to others' messages. These same factors help pastors receive others' nonverbal communication.[3] Our bodies are vehicles of communication. They signal the quality of our presence. Bodily attending communicates that we care for and respect our parishioners. They suggest that we are investing ourselves in others.

Eye contact is such a familiar term that it hardly needs any definition. Looking the other person in the eye is part of a communication process and frequently prompts persons to reciprocate, establishing eye contact. Shy persons tend not to take the initiative in making eye contact. Pastors can try too hard to establish eye contact, which gives the impression that they are staring. Some persons do not tolerate much eye contact. Usually, however, pastors discover that good eye contact enriches their understanding of what others are communicating because much is picked up through others' eyes and facial expressions. When pastors look people in the eye, parishioners usually interpret such behavior as a sign that pastors care and are ready to help. Contrariwise, when pastors are preoccupied or to a significant degree are uninterested in persons and their concerns, they are less likely to maintain frequent eye contact. There are times, however, when pastors who do care fail to maintain effective eye contact. Pastors who may care but are hooked on the content of what others say concentrate on interpreting in their own minds what others are communicating and so look down and to the side frequently in order to concentrate. This aids thought at the cost of communicating clearly that they care. Other pastors become absorbed in formulating what they will say in response to what they hear and consequently they frequently look away from parishioners. Though it will never do to suppose that one can manufacture a spirit of caring if it is not present, pastors should be alert to their nonverbal signals, including eye contact, because through habit, preoccupation, or being influenced by parishioners' behavior pastors may fall short of communicating to others a caring commitment that indeed is genuine.

Open posture here simply means having one's arms and legs uncrossed. Such posture suggests, at least unconsciously, to others that one is interested, even intensely interested and involved. Leaning toward persons and facing them squarely, in contrast to facing sideways or at an off angle, signal involvement and readiness to communicate. Pastors who tolerate conventionality and boredom well feel little need to face people squarely and openly because they have little need to invite more interesting and meaningful levels of communication. Of course, the reverse may be true: the pastor may be eager for more significant communication while others are not responsive to those nonverbal signals that demonstrate his or her readiness to know and understand at deeper levels. Pastors who are alert to these factors and who frequently engage parishioners in conversation in their studies arrange their studies so that no desk or table blocks bodily communication. By being aware of posture, pastors can assess their own level of involvement with parishioners and in light of circumstances decide whether the signs of their interest accord with their intentions. A pastor who is touched by a personal comment from a parishioner but knows that he plans to begin corporate worship in five minutes is not likely to exhibit all the signs of his felt concern.

A convenient way to make telling observations with respect to nonverbal behavior is to watch an interview or a panel discussion on television with the sound off. Observe the nonverbal behavior in detail. What nonverbal clues suggest to you that one person is listening to another? You can share your observations with a family member. Once you have done this, you can watch a similar program, but this time turn the sound on after a few minutes. You will be ready to observe what specific nonverbal behaviors complement what is being said and what behaviors detract from or seem to belie what is being said. It is helpful to observe both congruence and incongruence, i.e., communications in which the verbal and nonverbal messages synchronize and communications in which they conflict or at least do not augment each other well. Still, it is important that you pay especially close attention to congruent communication so that you have a model of how you hope to communicate.

Taken to the point of self-preoccupation, awareness of nonverbal, attending behaviors is counterproductive. That is, by becoming too concerned with such matters pastors diminish the actual attention they give to others. An awareness that is present yet "off to the side" as it were, does not interfere with communicating involvement with others. Such awareness of one's own bodily behavior works in harmony with awareness of one's emotional responses to other persons. For example, a pastor became aware of boredom in herself, then noticed that the person she was listening to spoke in a flat, monotonous voice. Wondering how much she had let her own behavior be influenced by this flatness, she intentionally leaned forward as part of her attempt to become more attentive. Soon the monotone voice gave way to a varied tonality that demonstrated the parishioner's vitality and involvement.

Pastors are influenced by others' behavior. Especially when persons are discouraged about their problems or when they have developed a tendency to depreciate themselves, they may relate nonverbally in ways that do not invite involved responses from others. Pastors who are passive, easily influenced by others, and not intentional in their behavior may then respond in ways that are in line with others' diminished expectations. Awareness of nonverbal behavior can help pastors address the issue of what their intentions and hopes for pastoral relationships are and help them identify when they fall short of representing the enduring and consistent love of God for his people. One should not presume, then, that by mechanically producing the nonverbal behaviors mentioned here, pastors will create personal involvement *ex nihilo*. On the other hand, a measure of self-awareness alongside involved caring for others helps pastors to ascertain how they are communicating their involvement as well as how they and others are influencing one another nonverbally.

Perhaps you have had conversations similar to the one above. In any case, you can probably recall with some vividness a significant conversation you have had within the past week. Imaginatively relive this experience, but picture yourself as bodily attending in a more complete way. See yourself doing this in a relaxed and spontaneous manner. Dwell on this image for a few minutes and also envision how your bodily communication might stimulate vitality in your parishioner's conversation.

So that you can apply these guidelines to your own ministry, let me ask you to examine your study or the place where you converse most often with people in your work. Can anything be rearranged to enhance attending and other aspects of nonverbal communication as you meet with a parishioner or a family? Do you have a place to sit so that you are in full view and not cut off by a desk or table between you and them? Are symbols of the faith tastefully present in the room? Take time to note the arrangements in the studies of a few of your colleagues in the ministry and discuss your ideas with them.

By now you may be in a position to assess your own communication style. Which of the elements of bodily attending characterize your conversations? Which one needs some attention on your part? It is important to select one only and give yourself some time to introduce it into your conversations to a noticeable extent as it seems appropriate to you. Give this a try for a week or two. Can you discern any difference in the interaction between you and others that appears to correlate with this change? Are you able to make the change without putting so much effort into it that you lose concentration on what and how others communicate to you? Does the change help you to receive more of others' communication? Does it enhance your readiness to listen totally to others? Are you able to make the change and still be spontaneous in your interactions with others?

ACCURACY

By definition empathy assumes accuracy of understanding. Thus Egan's phrase "accurate empathy" is redundant.[4] Even so, the theme of accuracy requires development. Parroting another's words assures accuracy, but others may feel that such responses are condescending. Accordingly, a rule of thumb with respect to accuracy is that responses should use different words but be interchangeable with what the person has said. A parishioner complains to a pastor about her father's hostile attitude toward her, "I feel damned if I do and damned if I don't," and the pastor responds, "You feel trapped and condemned." This slice of conversation would make sense if the parishioner had said, "I feel trapped and condemned," and the pastor had responded, "You feel damned if you do and damned if you don't." The pastor's response is interchangeable with what the person has said. Such accuracy is necessary to, but not sufficient for, empathy.

With respect to accuracy, three responses can be compared readily. A pastor's response may virtually repeat what a parishioner has just said. This is a parroting response. Certainly it is accurate, yet frequent parroting responses may contribute to parishioners' feeling that pastors are patronizing them. A second type of response closely resembles what the parishioner has said, but embodies the parishioner's message in the pastor's own words, and so does not parrot. This kind of response clearly is interchangeable with the parishioner's message. A third kind of response picks up on an implicit message in the statement or expresses what the pastor thinks is the person's message, though it is a matter of interpretation. This kind of response may pick up on a critical theme ensconced in the parishioner's message, yet its interchangeability may or may not be evident. As an example, a parishioner says, "I must not lose hope, but must keep fighting." A parroting response is "You have to keep fighting and not give up hope." The same message in the pastor's own words might be "No surrender now; you've got to keep trying." A response that is a bit more interpretive, in that it picks up on an implicit message, might be "Sounds as if you're thinking that your own determination is everything right now."

Parishioners' perceptions and feelings differ from their pastors' own perceptions and feelings. Pastors have responsibility to try not to confuse the two. This means that they need to be aware of their own responses to what is communicated to them, temporarily set aside their own viewpoint in order to communicate understanding to others, and acknowledge others' feelings as "true for them." If pastors are to be considered trustworthy, these disciplines are essential. Being aware of one's feelings helps to keep one's own needs from dictating the course of pastoral conversations. How pastors respond emotionally reflects in part their own needs at the moment. Responding to others on the basis of these needs may not be helpful. A pastor visited an elderly person who complained that he did not visit as soon as promised. Responding on the basis of a need for approval, the pastor defended himself and did not try to understand what underlay the complaint. Because she took delight in a parishioner's success, a pastor was quick to express delight at her promotion on the job. In doing so, however, the pastor missed responding to the tone of voice that suggested the parishioner's apprehension. Unwittingly the pastor communicated a message that advised, "Go with the positive feelings and hope the negative ones will go away." Had the pastor differentiated between her own feelings and expectations and the actual message, including the anxiety, she would have been prepared to help the person explore her situation and outlook. The task of being aware of one's own feelings and distinguishing them from the parishioner's is part of a moral commitment to serve. The capacity to be aware of one's personal response and differentiate it from the parishioner's way of seeing self and situation is a prerequisite to accuracy.

Because accuracy is not readily or easily reached, pastors should be appropriately tentative when communicating empathy. In part this is a matter of honesty and modesty. Pastors do not communicate respect when they presume to understand people better than these persons understand themselves. How much better to be tentative—e.g., "It sounds as though you are really fed up with the situation." Nor is it helpful for pastors to pretend to understand better than they in fact do. When pastors do not understand at all, they had best admit it and not fake understanding—e.g., "I'm afraid that I don't yet understand. Could you say some more?" People tolerate bungled attempts at empathy better than the presumption of understanding. Pastors can respond in ways that invite people to confirm or correct misunderstanding. The response "I know what you mean" does not invite confirmation or correction. A questioning tone of voice or a statement followed by a question, such as "Am I hearing you right?" communicates that the pastor wants to understand accurately and does not want to distort what the other person is saying. When a parishioner's message is forceful and clear, pastors need not respond tentatively, as if they followed a pat formula. Even so, genuine empathy emerges from a perspective that recognizes how elusive communication is. There are two sides to this difficulty. On the one hand, to project oneself imaginatively into the experience of another person is a complex task. On the other, people usually clarify their perceptions and feelings step by step as they give expression to them. Consequently, people may say one thing at one moment but shortly come to a more accurate expression of how they feel. Tentativeness gives people freedom to explore and clarify. Diligence in checking on the accuracy of one's perceptions of what people try to communicate combines with tentativeness to convey a sense of respect for the person.

Some empathic responses focus on what persons communicate explicitly. When pastors respond empathically to what is explicitly conveyed they are more likely to be accurate and to be responding to what persons are ready to explore. On the other hand, in most communication some feelings and perceptions are expressed vaguely and indirectly. They are intimated, not stated. Yet these feelings and perceptions may be as critical to an accurate understanding of persons as are the explicit messages. They cannot be avoided without an increased risk of misunderstanding. The skills approach to counseling psychology generally advocates that empathic responses at the early stage of exploration be limited to what people communicate explicitly and that attempts to communicate understanding of what persons hint at should be reserved for a second stage of a counseling relationship after trust has been established and the client has had the opportunity to explore her or his subjective feelings.[5]

How well does this guidance fit the pastoral situation? It is true that empathic responses to what persons explicitly say is a sensible way to begin. Often, however, pastors seek to help in relationships where trust has long been established and the pastors know the people quite well. In these situations pastors can respond to both explicit and implicit messages. Frequently pastors' conversations are one-time consultations. There is no need to prolong the exploration in deference to a counseling model that assumes numerous sessions on a regular basis. Pastors are likely to find it helpful to maintain a rhythm between responding to the explicit element in what people communicate and responding to the implicit element. The implicit dimension usually represents what they themselves are just beginning to consider or areas they are testing to determine whether they can discuss their concerns freely with their pastor. People move to new territory when pastors respond accurately to implied communication, but they may not be able to sustain that exploration and need recourse to what they can accept and own in an intentional way. Accordingly, pastoral care requires a readiness to be flexible in proceeding to explore new and demanding considerations or in reviewing and consolidating clear self-understandings. In any case, all that has been said about tentativeness above is underlined when pastors respond to the implicit aspects of people's conversations.

A middle-aged woman's husband was killed when his pickup

truck and an automobile collided at an intersection. The accident happened just after she had lunched with her husband at home. Reflecting back on that day she sighed and said, "If only I hadn't asked him to come home for lunch that day." The pastor picked up on the implicit feelings of guilt: "You're thinking that if only you had known, you could have prevented his death." She went on to talk about her feelings of guilt, though she knew they were irrational: "A part of me knows that it is silly to feel guilty, but if I hadn't so selfishly insisted on his spending time with me at lunch, it never would have happened." The pastor responded to another implication: "You feel guilty, but you recognize how senseless it is, because in fact you did not cause his death and could not have prevented it." She went on to identify her experience at a deeper level: what was so hard for her to accept was the utter helplessness that she felt. The feelings of irrational guilt helped her temporarily to avoid the painful feelings of helplessness, for the guilt feelings gave her the luxury of imagining that she had some responsibility. Guilt implies that she could have done something. To think of a way that she could have prevented the death was a way of denying the death. This is an understandable defense in a crisis. In this instance, the pastor knew that this person had managed much of her emotional denial and was ready to engage more deeply in the grief process. His responses to what she implied bore out his judgment about her readiness. It could have been otherwise. Had she not assimilated what he said and advanced with it, he would have needed to continue by responding to what she explicitly said. Such flexibility also would have shown respect for her own growth process.

THE CORE MESSAGE

The pastor's empathic task is to look for the person's core message. If the person is celebrating, what does that person perceive to be the basis for joy? If the person is exploring a problem, what is the nub of the person's concern—on what does it all seem to rest? If pastors respond to everything persons say, sentence by sentence as it were, their responses will not reflect any emerging pattern and will not be founded on thoughtful, sensi-

tive consideration. While spontaneity is important, it is also crucial that pastors discipline themselves to discern within the whole
of what people communicate a bottom line that discloses their
present orientation and that promises to lead to their fundamental outlook on life. Pastors who are able to get at the core message
intuitively relate content to feelings expressed. To respond to
content alone or to feelings alone often falls short of helping
persons to articulate their own message.

In a conversation with a woman, a pastor noticed that she
became very angry at one point. The anger surfaced in connection with a particular phrase that the parishioner's mother had
used. They had been discussing the impending divorce of the
parishioner's brother and she was explaining to her mother that
she was not in favor of the divorce, as somehow her mother had
assumed. When she explained her reasoning, her mother replied,
"Yes, you're always making decisions on such lofty considerations." The word "lofty" and the manner in which it was
spoken provoked the anger. When the parishioner went over this
conversation with the pastor, he responded, "It was that comment
about 'lofty considerations' that really got to you, it seems." This
response helped her explore further her relationship with her
mother and what was at stake for her in the way she heard her
mother's comment. Here the pastor connected feeling with a
particular content, which helped his parishioner progress toward
deeper self-understanding.

A practical way to reflect on the phenomenon of core messages
is to examine your own preaching. Select a recent sermon you
have preached that is recorded or has a written manuscript. Does
the conclusion really capture the essence of what you are trying to
say? Whether or not it does, write out in fresh words the core
message. If your sermon is complex, what gives it unity? What is
the sermon's highest priority, and how clearly does it stand out?
Often ministers discover that writing out a core message is difficult. If so, this may help you appreciate how involved the task of
communicating clearly is, and likewise how intricate the task of
listening for core messages is.

As far as the core message is concerned, the pastor may tend to respond too frequently or too infrequently. Responding too frequently can distract parishioners from concentrating on what they are trying to communicate. Furthermore, some persons may get the impression that the pastor is anxious or impatient. Listening intently to a parishioner describe his divorce, a pastor said, "You're angry." The parishioner acknowledged that he had been angry at the time and was ready to say more, but the pastor asked, "Why were you angry?" This question was not needed to help the person explore his concerns, and the parishioner felt that the pastor was being pushy. On the other hand, infrequent response can be problematic, for when this happens parishioners find themselves giving monologues and often they ramble rather than progress to the core of their concerns.

CONCRETENESS

Pastors' ability to help bring core messages to the surface can be considered further by reflection on concreteness. Effective pastors are alert to the varying levels of concreteness and vagueness that characterize conversations. The degree to which people are specific in what they say reflects the level of trust and indicates readiness to entertain actual change in behavior or orientation. The ability to help people speak more tangibly is not empathy, but it works well in tandem with empathy, because it nurtures trust and aids clarity. Pastors work so much with the broad and general concepts of faith and meaning that frequently they do not pursue the manifestations of such ideas in everyday details. But God's love took on concrete human form in Jesus Christ. Also, God's esteeming of us does not have a rider that lists conditions of worthiness. Hence, we need not save our own honor by resorting to generalities but are free to be concrete about all aspects of our lives. A sense of self-esteem that relies on the ability to be vague about oneself is vulnerable indeed. A strong esteem based on a grasp of how God esteems us can afford to express itself concretely in the context of a caring and thoughtful human relationship. Such concreteness can help persons with an idealized self-perception to become more realistic and self-accepting in a tough-minded way. When applied to awareness of one's

strengths, concreteness can help persons who otherwise under-
rate themselves to develop a substantive and balanced sense of
what they bring to their relationships. Unfortunately, the factor
of concreteness is often overlooked in pastoral communication.

Readiness to be concrete is a necessity in pastoral conversations
that are vehicles of growth in understanding or change. Concreteness is an indicator of the trust level that marks a relationship, and at the same time strengthens that trust. People who
trust each other become concrete in very short order. Most people
test the waters until they feel ready to risk being specific about
their experiences. That is why many conversations start out in
generalities. In response to a pastor's polite inquiry about how
things are going, a parishioner answers, "Pretty good," or
perhaps, "Not so good." Compare the following: "No big upsets
this week, and on top of that I got a good quarterly review at work,
so it's been a good week"; or, "My stomach has been sore and has
really flared up twice this week. It's my barometer for stress, so I
know that things are not so good." What matters is that pastors be
aware of the movement in relationships: Does communication
move from a somewhat vague level to conversations that introduce particulars, or does it stay at the same level of exploration?
As what point does a conversation that had been tangible subtly
become vague? Such a shift may signal sensitive areas. Persons
may be concrete about many areas in their lives but become vague
when they fear that the pastor may touch an emotional nerve. On
the other hand, concreteness may indicate both trust and a personal readiness to come to terms with what one is exploring. As
one adage had it, "What people can talk about they can manage in
principle."

Reflect on a recent conversation you have had that lasted more
than fifteen minutes. Did it progress step by step from general to
specific levels of communication? Or did it seem only to touch
momentarily anything specific? To what do you attribute its shifts
in levels of concreteness? Was there a retreat to generalities?
Why? Compare the first few minutes and the last few minutes of
this conversation. What were the significant differences?

The ability and willingness to be concrete helps persons to

anchor self-understanding. People often interpret their problems and patterns of dealing with life with ease and even sophistication, but if the insight does not entail a concrete description of themselves and their situation, it is not likely to produce genuine reconciliation or behavioral change. At one level of exploration, a woman parishioner said, "I've got talent and I know it and like to show it. It's not terribly humble, but I like to lead, do a superior job, and get recognized for it. It's not enough that I know I do excellent work. Everyone else has to recognize it or I'm angry and restless." At a more specific level she came to say, "I want everyone to acknowledge my leadership abilities, and especially right now I want Mary and Alice to compliment me. If they praise me I know I'm the best. It's hard for me to acknowledge this, but the fact is, I want them in particular—because they are so talented themselves—to be jealous of me." At this level she was facing herself squarely and was more ready to begin to work through a problematic area in her self-concept and interpersonal relations. Concreteness anchors understanding, intensifies it, and prepares a person for genuine change in identifiable ways. General insights foster self-satisfaction and produce little change.

How can pastors help persons explore their lives with greater concreteness? It is difficult to encourage concreteness, of course, if pastors do not exhibit the quality on their own side of the conversation. Pastors begin to foster concreteness by modeling it. When pastors state their purposes and role in specific terms, they help people to respond concretely. For example, when a person presented a personal problem, a pastor responded, "Let's take about an hour now, if you can, to explore this concern. I like to try to help first by simply understanding—looking at all this from your vantage point. Tell me what you can, and let's see if I can understand." Here the pastor proposed a time frame the person could accept or reject, and indicated her own approach to being helpful, at least in terms of getting started. Consequently, the parishioner knew what to expect, and since he agreed that the approach promised to be helpful, was ready to proceed with some expectation of how the pastor would respond. In short, as pastors declare their intentions, approaches, and feelings, people are more likely to trust them and become specific in the course of exploring their concerns. It is vital that pastors be very intentional about how they initiate conversations. Every once in a while it is a good idea to write out briefly how you will open a conversation. How clear can you be about your purpose and expectations in initiating your conversations?

As part of modeling concreteness, pastors should avoid cliches and similar generalizations: "We all have our faults that get to us now and then," "We have nothing to fear but fear itself." Since the first place that the significant modeling of concreteness occurs is the pulpit, you do well to assess the level of concreteness expressed in your preaching. Again, it is best to examine a manuscript or tape recording in order to let yourself be confronted with the details. Is your intent clear? Are your ideas advanced with representative examples and specific references? By listing particular changes that would improve the level of concreteness in this sermon, you make notes you can use in the preparation of future sermons.

Many pastors try to increase the level of concreteness in their conversations by asking questions. Usually these questions function as substitutes for statements. Pastors can translate many of their questions into statements and ask themselves if they really want to make these statements. Even though posed in the form of a question, the message is heard as a statement. From his conversation with a youth, a pastor had the impression that the youth felt intimidated and asked, "Do you feel intimidated by your parents?" He could just as well have said, "I sense that you feel intimidated. Is that on target?" When a young adult had an insight into the way he acted out his feelings toward his father by being late and admitted that he did this with others as well, the pastor responded, "Who needs to hear that? Do you think Janice needs to hear that?" This was a leading question. Straightforwardly put, the message was "I believe it would help your wife understand, if you shared this insight with her." Pastors who cannot own statements get nowhere by hiding behind questions.

There are situations when pastors must probe. At their best, pastors put a hold on their curiosity and probe only when they feel they must. Most probing questions can be open-ended, i.e., they are not answered properly in one word only. Closed questions are answered with one word, e.g., yes, no, or maybe. Open-ended questions, such as "How do you feel?" or "What did you make of that?" invite persons to fill in the gaps in their own way, and unlike closed questions, are not so likely to exclude data that pastors cannot foresee may need attention. The leading question "Did this have anything to do with what happened between the two of you last year?" checks on one possibility only and excludes many others. The question "What do you feel is going on here?" invites this couple's own interpretations.

Of course, there are situations in which a direct question is necessary or at least advisable. Many clergy who could help explore a drinking problem simply do not bring it up even when there are signs that people may be struggling with this problem. Again, whether a person who is depressed is contemplating suicide may need to be asked.

In personal conversations certain aspects of our experiences are amplified and others are muted. What persons regularly hide or avoid, communicates something significant about them. To become sensitive to what is amplified and what is toned down in communication, pastors can ask three questions about the messages they receive: What did the person say? What did the person not say? What did the person mean? To further refine their attention to the concrete dimensions of what people are communicating pastors can keep in mind four categories: happening, action, feeling, and meaning. The first term refers to whatever people perceive as happening to them. Action refers to what people do. Feeling refers to the emotional response to events that give shape to what people do. Meaning refers to the significance people ascribe to what happens to them, and to their actions and feelings. A woman says, "He made me angry." She construes the event as a happening in that she portrays an outside event, what someone else did, as the cause for her feelings. She does identify her feeling. In this brief statement she does not address what she did in response to his behavior, only how she felt. Nor does she elaborate on the significance that his action had for her, or the meaning of her anger. In other words, in her brief sentence, two of the four categories are present and two are absent. Pastors should not assume they have heard the full story until they have a well-textured account that includes all four dimensions. Observant pastors will discern patterns in what people communicate readily and what they avoid. Some people relay to others only what happens to them. They do not depict their own action, before or after what has happened. They relate to others and to life passively. In all likelihood, these persons will avoid responsibility by relating passively to pastors too. Others are vague about what happens to them, including how others respond to them, but they speak concretely about what they themselves do or how they feel. Their lack of mutuality centers on their own activity to such a degree that they are insensitive to others' behavior and messages. One can readily see how these persons may ignore what pastors say or do. With one person who often was vague about her perceptions, a pastor said, "I sense that you are very angry. It would help me to understand, if you could tell me more about what happened." The anger that had come through loud and clear was not new because this parishioner was frequently angry. The pastor wanted a clearer sense of what happened before judging whether the anger was out of proportion to the event.

Other persons are articulate about what happens to them and how they react, but they do not attend to their feelings. Pastors are at a loss to identify the feeling by attending to either their words or their nonverbal signals. It seems these persons have established a working distance between their perceptions or actions and how they feel.

Finally, some people fall short of spelling out the bottom line of meaning. They tend to see the parts but do not constructively bind them together in a meaningful whole. Frequently pastors try to nudge persons to engage in this task by asking *why* questions: "Why do you suppose you feel so strongly about this?" There is a place for such inquiry in pastoral conversations, but it is important that pastors not short-circuit the process by advancing to *why* questions before the emotions have been felt deeply and before the *what* and *how* questions have been examined. Otherwise, people will be allowed to settle for quick insights that slight significant facts and feelings. On the other hand, pastoral conversations are exceptional opportunities for people to reexamine the issues of meaning and faith in their lives. Pastors should be ready to take pains with this fundamental dimension of what persons bring to them, whether or not it is elaborated in religious language.

Meanings are particularly important in pastoral care, for meanings articulate people's faith. When meanings are taken seriously, pastoral ministry goes beyond mere catharsis of emotions. When people disclose the meanings beyond their feelings, actions, and perceptions, they reveal much about themselves: how generous they may be, how insecure or secure, how self-serving or accepting. At the same time, people use interpretations to avoid facing themselves, save face, or depreciate themselves. While pastors are called to understand people's representations of themselves, they are not called to concur with the meanings people assign to their own behavior, perceptions, and feelings. Since the relation of meaning to these other dimensions of personal experience needs consideration, pastors can help people make these connections. At times people present themselves as confused with regard to meaning. Often pastors are in a position to know whether this is a long-time stance toward life by which they are avoiding issues of faith, or is a time of transition, and possibly transformation, during which old meanings will give way to new ones. Sometimes people's thoughts and attitudes are simply irrational, and they recognize this fact when pastors prompt them to examine how they interpret their experience. At other times people come to see that their particular interpretations do not match what they profess to believe or have learned about Christian faith. The main point here is that concreteness is not the enemy of meaningfulness. To the contrary, by nurturing concreteness in what persons perceive to happen, their actions, and their feelings, as well as in the meanings that permeate their experience, pastors usually can help people make their own connections, thereby finding new perspectives and coming to new decisions.

When people reexamine their beliefs in relation to their experiences and their experiences in light of their faith, the emergence of images is a good indicator of concreteness. It is difficult to relate the whole and the parts of one's life without resorting to images and analogies. These images have power to synthesize. The Psalms have concreteness because of their rich imagery, in which particular events, behaviors sparked by feeling and patterned to yield meaning, take on a double significance, for they constitute an identifiable segment of a person's life, like a paragraph, and at the same time, like a chapter, stand for a larger movement in that person's life. When persons converse with pastors, their concrete references often have this symbolic meaning—that is, an entire story or a whole outlook on life may be compressed into the concrete imagery they use. When pastors look for concreteness in people's communications, they help them to listen for living symbols. In the following a parishioner becomes aware of the symbolic dimension of an event in his life:

> Pastor, I'm beginning to see that I'm bored much of the time. I've complained off and on about the routine at work and the lack of fun in my life. Last night Joanie and I went out to dinner at one of our favorite places. We sat there, enjoying the food in a way, yet not saying anything. To me it was not a comfortable silence. It's not that we have to talk all the time, but I was bored and I tolerated it, pacified by the food. It terrifies me to realize that I have become so tolerant of boredom. I've come to accept it at work, in my marriage . . . everywhere. It seems like a small price to pay for the comforts of my life, yet I'm afraid of what I have let happen to me. I guess there's a rebel in me that leers at this treaty I've signed with conventionality.

This man focused on an event, going out to dinner with his wife, as a symbol of all that was happening in his life. Also, concrete images, such as the signing of a peace treaty, dramatized his feelings about losing a sense of adventure in life.

Before proceeding, I am going to ask you to give yourself a bonus by making use of your ability to be concrete. Think back on your life, recalling particular people who have had an impact on your own development of character. Select one whom you see as an outstanding model of interpersonal communication. In your mind picture this person listening to others and talking with them. When you feel ready, make a list of this person's communication abilities. Avoid general or vague terms. Challenge yourself to be as specific as you possibly can. The bonus you have given yourself is a concrete model of a caring communicator.

GENUINENESS

To consider the meaning of genuineness, ask yourself how you determine whether someone genuinely intends to help you. For what specific clues do you look in order to decide if the person has your best interest in mind? Recalling a particular incident, identify clues to genuine commitment to your welfare and to lack of such commitment. Can similar features in yourself be useful indicators of how genuine you are in your efforts to be helpful in your pastoral ministry? Keep in mind these data from your own experience as you consider further the place of genuineness in pastoral conversations.

In both client-centered and skills approaches to counseling, genuineness on the part of the counselor is understood to be a condition that facilitates personal growth. Of course, genuineness is hardly just a skill. One genuinely cares or one does not. On the other hand, it is possible that one genuinely cares yet fails to communicate this spirit to others. Furthermore, people make inference about genuineness in others on the basis of various behavioral clues. This does not mean that genuineness can be reduced to a behavioral formula that can be imitated. Still, how genuineness is communicated can be described in concrete ways. The meaning of genuineness is not exhausted by any behavioral list, but genuineness has its behavioral manifestations, some of which may be said to be highly characteristic expressions of genuineness.

To be genuine is actually to possess the reputed or apparent qualities. When this definition from *Webster's New Collegiate Dictionary*[6] is applied to pastors, it means that they not only appear to care but also in fact do care. The main image that depicts this definition is of the way objects or persons may accord with an original type without counterfeiting. The theme of genuineness points pastors, then, to the original ministry of Jesus Christ, who is the model and power for the church's ministry and the ordained ministry. Frequently people have distorted images of Jesus Christ and, consequently, improper expectations of ordained ministers. The issue is not whether ministers conform to these expectations but whether they genuinely reflect the spirit of Jesus' ministry. At this point we are directed to a reality that precedes our own participation in it and to a process of coming to know that reality in deed as well as word. No minister perfectly represents Jesus Christ, yet genuine allegiance to him exists. Genuineness is more than sincerity, which may be utterly naive. Genuineness entails informed commitment as a response to divine grace. For pastors genuineness is the gift of being free from pretense, and it is the gift of representing the gospel of Christ without hypocrisy in a blend of pastoral office and personhood. As well as any persons, pastors should be able to realize that their love and care of others is not grounded solely in themselves or their own inner experience. When genuine, pastors avoid parading either their role as clergy or their personalities. But neither do they deny their role or personhood.

Various ways of exaggerating one's status as a clergyperson can block the effective communication of genuine caring. Pastors do this when they hold up a Bible between themselves and the persons they are with, when they habitually pray aloud with persons regardless of the spirit and dynamics of their conversations, when they compulsively steer the conversation to overtly religious matters, and when they convey a moral or spiritual superiority to the persons they profess to serve. An exaggerated sense of role sometimes causes pastors to be preoccupied with whether their responses fit professional standards, and this preoccupation diminishes their spontaneity. Pastors' status and actions are not meant to be vehicles of power over people or veils that keep their vulnerability out of view. Though there is no great virtue in parading one's weaknesses, to hide one's vulnerabilities because one is an ordained minister conveys a lack of self-acceptance that is inconsistent with the gospel. Exaggeration of role tends to communicate self-importance, not caring.

On the other hand, readiness to be somewhat low-keyed with respect to one's authority as a minister does not mean that pastors should pretend that they have no role. This denial entails as much falsehood as any parading of oneself as an ordained minister. Again, when pastors introduce psychological jargon into their conversations more frequently than religious language, people begin to wonder about their genuineness. For this and similar reasons Paul Pruyser admonishes ministers to use their own vocabulary but to do so without imposing religious language where it is not well understood. Ministers ought not to rely primarily on specialized vocabularies from outside the religious tradition they represent. Such counsel does not at all suggest that pastors cannot learn from psychological disciplines. If they rely primarily on these sources for their self-understanding and functioning, however, they jeopardize their ability to convey genuineness.

Pastors who neither deny nor exaggerate their role are in a position to understand the need for balance between planned, disciplined responses to persons and spontaneity. On the one hand, pastors who care do not want to verbalize everything that comes to mind. The value of spontaneity is not a license for indiscriminate behavior. These pastors select how they respond to what people say and do. On the other hand, pastors who mull over every word sacrifice spontaneity and can come across as so cautious that people wonder if they care. While the pastoral role is not to be forsaken, ministers in the course of pastoral work come to know people as persons and people come to know ministers as persons. The responses of caring pastors exude energy because they allow the personalities of the pastors to show through.

Consistency is another mark of genuineness. I refer here to more than consistency between what pastors say one minute and what they say the next. The concept includes what Carl Rogers called congruency, or consistency between what one says and how one says it, i.e., between the verbal and nonverbal messages. Rogers suggests that counselors not express negative feelings to clients unless these feelings persist to the point of interfering with their ability to help.[7]

A persisting disjunction between communicating a sense of care and harboring feelings such as dislike and disapproval erodes genuineness. How different this is from a movement from inconsistency to consistency as a pastoral relationship develops. This segment from a pastor's conversation illustrates the point:

> Parishioner: Pastor, I want you to know that I found myself right on the edge of my seat during your sermon last Sunday when you were talking about the Pope's visit to Central America. I appreciate what you had to say.
>
> Pastor: Oh, I wish I could have said it better. It's such a delicate and complex matter . . . (pause) Do you realize what is happening right now? We've been working on your tendency to express only negative comments and keep buried the legitimate warm feelings within you. You just gave me a simple compliment and I started to shrug it off.

The pastor began to respond only to content and was not mindful of the whole situation being addressed in her ministry with this person. Correcting herself, however, she acknowledged her inconsistency at verbally encouraging the expression of positive feelings yet cutting off attempts at such expression. In this response she showed spontaneity as well as self-acceptance, and moved toward a more consistent style of relating to her parishioner.

When people are defensive, we think of them as not open to others' messages, as threatened, and perhaps as preoccupied with themselves. Defensiveness in pastors blocks the communication of genuineness because it demonstrates that, at least for the time, they are not open to others. In some respects, to avoid defensiveness is far more difficult for pastors than it is for psychotherapists. Pastors are leaders of congregations and frequently are the object of criticisms. Sometimes pastors are scapegoats when people have hurt feelings, which they bring to pastors in the form of an attack. How important it is that pastors curb the tendency to take matters personally when reality does not require that they do so. Actually, most pastors have just this tendency; they are sensitive and tend to assume that they had or have the power to make things better. Consequently, a criticism of a church program, though it was discussed and approved by a church committee, may nonetheless be taken personally. How difficult it is for pastors when someone who is disappointed and has difficulties coping with the welter of problems in his life has selected one from the many and comes to the pastor with both barrels loaded. The intensity that results from this person's many frustrations propels the particular complaint that he levels. How can pastors take such persons seriously, avoid being unduly defensive, and still get at the larger picture of what the persons are trying to resolve? Managing all these tasks is not always feasible, but pastors must always try not to be defensive. It helps if they can step back from the situation and ask the questions: What feelings move these persons to criticism? Who is the object of these feelings? Are their reactions appropriate to what they describe or what is known about the situation? If the persons are angry, do any other feelings accompany, or remain masked behind, this anger? What can be learned constructively from these criticisms that might improve our ministry? The following chapter will provide guidance about the manner in which confrontation may help move people beyond unjustified criticisms to more meaningful interpersonal relations and problem-solving.

COMMUNICATING RESPECT

The perspective informing this study highlights the role of respect vis-à-vis empathy and related communications skills that, like empathy, help to educe the person's own perspective and sense of responsibility. In counseling psychology literature, respect is approached as a value or skill along with empathy and genuineness. Given this somewhat narrower approach, I want to discuss the communication of respect, as a separable theme. In one sense, this section reinterprets from a pastoral viewpoint the psychological treatment of respect. In another sense, the concept "communicating respect" enlarges what has already been said about respect in relation to empathic communication and affords additional guidelines for communicating the pastor's respect for his or her parishioners.

Carl Rogers first developed the psychological concept of respect in the context of counseling. He understands respect, as he does genuineness, to be a condition that facilitates human growth,[8] and he attempts to describe respect or "unconditional positive regard" in concrete terms. Gerald Egan defines respect as "prizing others simply because they are human beings."[9] Romano Harre believes that respect is the fundamental need that characterizes human beings.[10] According to *Webster's New Dictionary of Synonyms*, "respect" belongs to a family of words that refer to recognition of worth and some degree of liking. Sometimes respect implies "a show of deference or veneration as is proper from a junior or an inferior. . . ."[11] The communication of respect in pastoral care may entail the reversal of social expectations, in which a professional person who is esteemed in the community regards another who may not have high reputation as a person of special and high worth. St. Paul's counsel that we esteem others higher than ourselves expresses the moral force of this dimension of ministry. The synonym "esteem" highlights the warmth of feeling that accompanies the high value attributed to one's personal worth.

Behaviors that embody respect are ways of communicating the attitude and value of respect for other persons. Pastors' availability and willingness to work with people communicate respect for them. Taking initiative in calling people and letting them know that the pastor is interested and available whenever help is needed is an example. Faithfulness in keeping appointments is another.

Pastors demonstrate regard for people's individuality when they resist temptations to mold parishioners in their own image. Imbued with high regard for people, pastors tend not to be directive, in the sense of advising people what to do, except for short-term guidance in crisis situations, when people's ordinary resourcefulness for coping with problems is diminished. In other words, within reasonable limits these pastors expect people to be responsible for how they handle their circumstances and for their decisions. One should note the demand quality of this expectation. Rogers' term "unconditional positive regard" does not imply that appreciating persons is a sentimental attitude that permits people to avoid reality or responsibility. Rather positive regard for persons as such makes "benevolent demands" of them, inviting them to relate to themselves with a positive attitude, and to reject destructive behaviors that deny personal worth. The communication of respect is both the recognition that persons have worth and the expectation that they will relate to themselves and others in light of this value. Their meeting this expectation is not a condition for continuing to relate to them but it does confront them with the possibilities of grace. This attitude helps people learn how not to condemn or reject themselves because of certain acts or faults, and encourages them to abandon attitudes not consistent with positive self-regard rooted in divine love and forgiveness. Toleration of irresponsibility, which may seem the easier route for pastors, is in fact opposed to positive regard and respect.

When respectful, pastors relate to persons as unique individuals. Respectful pastors do not label people either positively or negatively in ways that encourage stereotyping. Respect does not esteem persons artificially as far better than they in fact are. A good indicator of respect is a fascination with individuals, an interest in their distinctive qualities as well as in their particular stories and outlooks. Pastors are respectful when they show interest in persons as they are, neither putting them on pedestals nor running them down.

Respect implies more than that ministers resist the temptation to place conditions on persons' acceptability or worth. It implies that these persons have worth regardless of the conditions under which they face life, that is, their circumstances. From the standpoint of justice, this means that ministers not value the rich and those who are able to be more productive, over the poor and those who are less able to be productive. An attitude of respect appreciates persons' worth despite the fact that things may not work out well. To reassure people that everything will come out all right when this may not be the case often communicates to people that pastors do not regard them as strong in adversity. Typically, verbal reassurance that others are persons of good will is unnecessary and often is counterproductive. As noted at the beginning of this chapter, in the process of helping a parishioner face a choice about whether to follow a legal process in handling domestic violence, a pastor responded empathically, "It's hard to make a decision when you've been hurt by someone you love." Later the pastor said, "It's difficult, but I know you are sincere and will make the decision that is right for you." This comment communicated unnecessary reassurance, in that sincerity is no guarantee of the best choice. Often the communication of respect is reassuring in its effect on persons, yet respect is not reassurance in the sense of suggesting that everything will work out somehow. Indeed, sometimes respect communicates appreciation for the person's worth despite the fact that things may not work out well at all.

Respect for persons is also evident in pastors' awareness of their good will and interest in constructive change. Such respect does not deny that people often resist help and refuse to do much for themselves, but pastors committed to respecting persons are alert for any evidence of persons' good will and of their readiness, despite anxieties and adversities, to grow. Consequently, respect at times amplifies persons' awareness of their own constructive intent and dampens the destructive forces within them. As social encouragement for persons to be attuned to and not neglectful of the good will that is present and at work within them, the communication of respect should not distort reality but restore balance when persons with low self-esteem have lost contact with, or do not fully appreciate, constructive realities within them.

People need respect from others yet resist it when it conflicts with their own negative self-appraisal. At times these persons will seem to have the strategy of inducing you to show little or no respect for them. A creative response to this is to concentrate on how you can disengage such strategies and express your desire for a constructive, respectful relationship.

Initially, respect involves suspending critical judgments of persons. These negative evaluations are set aside, at least temporarily, in order that they not distract pastors from communicating their affirmation of the sacred worth of persons in their care. When persons are distressed already, communicating criticism, whether overt or subtle, discourages them from full exploration. At the beginning of a pastoral visit dealing with conflict between a mother and her teen-age daughter, a pastor noted that when the mother twice asked the daughter to justify her actions, the daughter simply let the mother's remarks slide by without a response. In the second instance the mother said, "Speaking of Jane, you haven't spent time with her in ages. What's wrong with her that you aren't friends anymore?" The pastor might have considered the daughter's silence a constructive attempt to prevent conflict from escalating to the point where it was unmanageable. Or the pastor might have seen this behavior as a fault. In any case, had the pastor said to the daughter, "It seems you don't stand up for yourself," he would have risked conveying a critical attitude toward her, not unlike the mother's attitude, and would not have demonstrated respect for her. At a later moment, when the pastor's respect for her is evident to the daughter, the pastor could confront her. Nor does the guideline that pastors suspend judgment mean that they are to abandon moral perspective. As Don Browning has emphasized, pastoral care proceeds on the assumption that the church is a community of moral discourse and provides a context that makes grace meaningful.[12] Suspending judgment does help pastors to maintain a respectful and objective spirit that opens up and enriches communication. Furthermore, the setting aside of critical judgments helps pastors to avoid the unwitting reinforcement of negative behaviors by paying undue attention to them.

To bring home the force of respect as unconditional positive regard, imagine that your best friend has been charged with intentional murder and is in jail. You are not familiar with the evidence in this case. Picture yourself visiting your friend and think how you will convey respect without implying that your respect is based on your knowing that your friend must be innocent.

Warmth communicates a sense of esteem. Touch and warmth in tone of voice convey a pastor's personal involvement. This style of communication contrasts with a distant, predominantly analytical attitude that skirts active participation in order to maintain objectivity. Pastors are responsible for a significant degree of objectivity, but this objectivity emerges along with their participation, for pastors are participant observers in a rhythmic process:

their observations enrich their participation and their participation provides varied data for careful reflection. Pastoral relationships involve ministers in the reality of personal knowledge wherein they come to know best what and whom they love best.[13] The basis for pastors' warmth is their caring and respect for persons. Warmth does not imply that pastors take sides with persons or agree with them, only that they recognize persons' worth as individuals. Keeping in mind the symbolic power of gesture, pastors can express warmth in concrete but modest ways. Pastors need to be especially judicious in expressing warmth to members of the opposite sex.

The variety of ways in which respect can be communicated through listening and empathy may be endless. The guidelines presented here demonstrate representative ways in which caring esteem for persons comes to expression. Pastors' empathic understanding helps persons to explore their situations and understand themselves, and may be the occasion for persons' coming to realize something of the immeasurable value God places on their lives. Now the question arises, Can confrontation, like empathy, also communicate deep and genuine respect? The next chapter explores this question.

CHAPTER 4

Confrontation and Respect

To move beyond borders of empathy to consider confrontation in pastoral ministry may appear to be like entering an alien land. The differences are striking. In empathic listening, the pastor's own viewpoint is held in check to assure accurate and caring understanding of the other person. In confrontation, a perspective other than the parishioner's own is introduced. Usually empathy helps people expand and develop what they themselves have introduced. While one may hope for readiness, confrontation ventures to help persons face facts or issues they may not want to consider. These contrasts have been dramatized so that the empathic and confrontational frequently are seen as two approaches to counseling. One adopts one approach or the other as the style of one's pastoral ministry. Or, in a more eclectic spirit, one adapts one style to one set of circumstances and the other style to other situations. Pastors discover, however, that each approach without the other is limited, if not handicapped. Some persons do not readily respond to caring empathy as they explore their problems. They seem unable or unprepared to do so. Others face situations so complex that it is unrealistic to expect them to discover within themselves all the resources and considerations that ought to be applied in facing their concerns. Even when understanding is advanced through empathy, the stimulation of an additional approach may be immensely helpful. On the other hand, confrontation that presumes to proceed without empathy often misses the mark as well as provoking unnecessary opposition and defensiveness. Even when confrontation is "successful" in that it produces a change in behavior, one can rightly wonder how deep and lasting the change is, not to mention at what cost emotionally the change was brought about. For example, a group may pressure an individual to admit a fault and believe it has helped this person to mature, but one may suppose that the person suppressed perceptions and feelings in the process of yielding to the group's collective wisdom. To adopt an empathic approach or a confrontational approach may simplify some aspects of the minister's work, but it generates problems as well.

While some styles of confrontation are incompatible with empathy, not all are. Respect is a moral connection that discloses how empathy and certain ways of being confrontive require each other. Respectful, considerate confrontation goes hand in hand with empathy. This is not the kind of confrontational attitude where one says, "It's my job to hit people between the eyes with reality, and what they do with it is their business." Rather, respectful confrontation communicates in essence, "Having gained some understanding of you, I now trust you to deal openly with some things you have not considered." That is, for all their differences, there is no fundamental contradiction when ministers who are empathic are also confrontational, so long as there is respect. Such an understanding of pastoral ministry is critical, if pastors are to be faithful to Christian tradition, including its ethical dimensions. Don Browning has highlighted these dimensions in a timely manner.[1] In part, the task of this chapter is to show that respect is a key concept for an insight into how pastors can invite people to give careful consideration to Christian wisdom and moral guidance.

We have examined some ways that respect is communicated when educing parishioners' perspective. The task now is to examine ways in which respect is communicated when parishioners are being challenged to consider others' perspectives.

The ordinary meanings of "confront" are to face, especially in challenge; to cause to meet, or bring face to face; to encounter. When confrontation develops from empathy, another perspective is added to what has been educed from parishioners. It well may be the pastor's own perspective that is introduced, or perspectives the pastor feels the person would do well to consider. Parishioners may welcome the opportunity to consider another perspective. They may find it stimulating and immediately helpful. Or they may not. In confrontation the possibility of conflict is present because there is more than one perspective. Some persons recoil from the idea of confrontation because for them it connotes conflict. Conflict is at least possible, and pastors who decide to be confrontive must realize that they make themselves vulnerable even as they make demands on others, for parishioners may challenge pastors' views or their manner of confrontation. Although people understandably associate confrontation and conflict, conflict is nothing new in the context of pastoral ministry, since people may resist empathic understanding from their pastors as well as confrontation. Persons who expect advice and confrontation may resist the expectation, implicit in empathy, that they will explore thoroughly their own experience. Or persons may resist any confrontation because they want and expect supportive reassurance. Nevertheless, when thinking of confrontation we ordinarily are especially alert to the possibility of conflict, since more than one perspective is out on the table.

In listening, pastors challenge persons to understand themselves. In confrontation, pastors challenge persons to be open to another view. The former, by entailing openness to oneself, nourishes sociality within oneself, for it stimulates inner dialogue. The latter extends this sociality toward openness to others, helping to complete the circle of sociality. Confrontation can be seen as a necessary form of helping if one understands the essential sociality of human life. No one can rely on self-understanding without the aid of others' ideas, feedback, and challenge, for the outside dimension is a vital resource to help correct systematic distortions to which any individual is subject. Donald Capps suggests that because vices distort self-understanding, confrontation is required.[2] Furthermore, when confrontation helps persons develop objectivity in self-examination, it also tends to strengthen the capacity for impartiality in relation to others, a capacity as integral to the moral life as fairness.[3]

Empathy alone, as a complete methodology of pastoral care, unwittingly fosters self-reliance in the extreme, and in doing this places an unwieldy burden on persons. In addition, listening alone often fails to challenge persons in their interpersonal relationships. By listening, pastors adapt themselves to others. When this posture is not balanced by challenging persons to consider others' perspective, it runs the risk of encouraging people to idolize their own self-understanding. In the context of pastoral care as a whole, listening helps people to be responsible for their experience and to clarify their problems. Furthermore, listening shows openness, for in being empathic, pastors exhibit openness to parishioners. They also serve as models for persons to be open to others. Genuine dialogue emerges when readiness to give careful consideration to one's own perceptions, feelings, and interpretations is joined by readiness to give careful consideration to others' perceptions, feelings, and interpretations. Confrontation, then, invites persons to extend and enrich their participation in community. Such participation in community is essential to the development of character and to the transformation of spirit. Commenting on the role of the pastor as a moral counselor, Donald Capps notes that for Erik Erikson virtues are "inherent strengths that are cultivated in encounter."[4]

Pastoral care prizes listening and empathy. At the same time pastoral care aims toward mutuality, but not a mutuality in which there is no division of labor or distinction of role. Nevertheless, the mutuality entails the hope of a partnership in which each is open to the other. The pastor represents a tradition that provides perspective on our tendencies to be culture-bound in understanding and communication. When faithful to persons and to our calling, our pastoral care relies on the promise that interpersonal perspectives will correct and enhance individual perspectives and also holds out the hope that both partners can be open to the possibilities of transcendence that are inherent in the Christian faith. In caring confrontation, pastors help persons to apply the grace and wisdom of Christian tradition. Thus confrontation serves to expand people's horizons by broadening the field of conversation to include spiritual and moral considerations. Such expansion should be undertaken respectfully and grow out of what was initially in view when listening was the primary mode of ministering.

Confrontation can be seen as a core concept around which cluster several skills, all of which promote the same purpose of inviting persons to consider others' perspectives openly. These elements belong together both by virtue of their common purpose and by virtue of the common moral tie, respect, that gives direction to the pastors' task of challenging persons. Respectful confrontation is faithful to the guidelines that help pastors to maintain and express esteem for persons.

The skills of confrontation give concrete expression to the respect necessary in pastoral relationships. Furthermore, these skills are one index of character development. That is, the skills can be learned, and a structured learning process will help in this, yet the process cannot be reduced to a mechanical routine. Readiness to confront constructively is an expression of character. The practice of techniques and skills strengthens capacity, but capacity is not the same as readiness. One may have capacity to confront constructively, yet under particular circumstances not have the courage. On the other hand, one may have the courage and the right intent, yet not the prudence to carry out confrontation in a thoughtful manner. In short, learning the following guidelines regarding confrontation will help pastors develop prudence in this area but will not yield all the virtues to which Christ in grace calls us. Practice of communication skills strengthens capacity, but practice does not answer the question of one's readiness to confront others. Pastors who find conflict especially demanding emotionally may be helped somewhat by the practice of skills, but the major task for them involves their spiritual and personal development over the long haul, and this may entail therapy.

Confrontational pastoral care can help persons to discover that judgment is a vehicle of grace. When faced with considering others' perspectives, which often entails some kind of self-assessment, parishioners may discover personal limitations, faults, shortcomings, and omissions that are difficult to face without a sense of the presence of God's grace. Respectful confrontation sounds a note of grace and can sustain persons by helping them to envision that grace is at work in the very moment when judgment calls.

CONFRONTATION

When challenging people, the pastor is like a host bringing two people together who need to talk out their differences. Sometimes this literally is the situation as pastors attempt to facilitate reconciliation between people. Sometimes pastors take the initiative when there is conflict between themselves and parishioners, trying to reestablish cooperative and close relationships. In these instances the pastors are like hosts at the same time that they are one of the parties to the conflict. At other times pastors are like hosts even though there are not two or more persons who need reconciliation but rather one person who faces a conflict within. Pastors can help such people negotiate with themselves. Often this hosting is the occasion that brings the persons in touch with previously unacknowledged aspects of their character or behavior. Carkhuff and Berenson see confrontation as directed toward discrepancies between a person's ideal and real self.[5]

Pastors should not take confrontation for granted. Like others, they need to earn the right to confront, after they have invested themselves, their time, and their effort into forming a caring relationship. Some pastors feel an urge to confront because they represent a moral point of view in the community. Indeed they do. Yet constructive confrontation is not stone-throwing. What pastors represent morally is already known and so does not need belaboring. Authority to teach spiritual truths and moral principles does not spare pastors the task of establishing trust and being empathic. A humane and unpretentious approach is in order. One pastor heard of an affair a parishioner was having. The pastor marched into the man's office at a bank, told him what he had heard, and demanded that the man call on the phone and end the affair immediately. The man was shocked and he complied. The pastor thought his confrontation was successful because it produced the results he wanted to see. But from my point of view, he owed his parishioner far more than this hit-and-run pastoral visit: he needed to communicate genuine care and to help the persons involved explore the situation in greater depth.

Caring confrontation is based on an accurate and well-founded understanding of the parishioner as a person. Consequently, confrontation without empathy can be unwittingly disrespectful and can be ineffective because it is based on inaccurate assumptions. Careful listening helps to assure that ministers have a reasonably informed view of a situation before they issue challenging interpretations or prescriptions. For this reason, the necessity of empathy is not limited to the need for trust in a relationship. Pastors may have earned people's trust, yet need an accurate picture of the situation in which they are called to help. Understanding the parishioner's experiences is an essential aspect of such understanding.

When pastors have parishioners' trust, their concerns can usually be explored readily so that pastors need not wait interminably, as if they were engaged in long-term therapy, before confronting. Consequently, empathy and confrontation can be placed together. A pastor met in counseling with a couple. The husband expressed bitter alienation, complaining that his wife constantly tried to control his life. After some careful listening to both persons, when the man reiterated his complaint, the pastor responded:

> You are really angry and fed up at what you see as Mary's attempts to dominate you. From what I've heard both of you say, I wonder at the same time if you yourself do not have a role in this problem. Could it be that you cast her in this role by letting things go that you are responsible for, until she tries to get you to act?

In this response the pastor took time to indicate that he was aware of the husband's feelings and point of view. He went on to raise a challenging question that invited the husband to examine his behavior from another point of view. This point of view does not ignore the husband's self-understanding, because even if correct, it may still be that the wife takes the bait and begins to exert control over him. That is, she is responsible too for her role in the drama. The expression of empathy helps to affirm that the husband's own experience is not being dropped or rejected out of hand, but the addition of the confrontive response suggests that his perspective is a partial one.

Pastors who take the risk of challenging others sometimes will be challenged in return. People may see pastors' confrontations as misinformed, and they may be right. Again, there is no place for defensiveness here. Because pastors are helping persons face reality, and are not facing it for them, pastors need not be inflexible about what they have offered for parishioners' consideration. Various feelings and perceptions may be examined with mutual openness before a trustworthy challenge to objective understanding is hammered out. Some pastors shun confrontation in order to avoid being challenged in return and to avoid embarking on the uncertainties of a conversation in which neither person's initial perspective will prevail.

Unfortunately, for many people the term "confrontation" connotes negative responses that point out people's inadequacies. Confrontation is hardly limited to these. The highest moments in confrontation come when pastors point out persons' strengths and assets and the resources that they are not using fully. Here pastors challenge people's potential. On the one hand, it is essential that pastors be honest in their assessments of persons' strengths. The tendency to idealize and "pretty up" the picture is a bane for a significant number of ministers. On the other hand, people do avoid responsibility by neglecting to acknowledge and make use of their strengths. When pastors point out persons' realistic potential, they instill renewed confidence and courage. According to Carkhuff and Berenson, "High-level functioning therapists confront both clients and patients with their assets and resources more often than they confront them with their limitations. On the other hand, low-level functioning therapists confront their clients and patients more often with their limitations than they do with their resources."[6] This may be an overstatement, but I do believe that the opportunity to challenge people on the basis of the strengths that pastors can affirm honestly is frequently missed.

A young woman told her minister how discouraged she felt about the lack of enthusiasm in the youth group she had begun to lead a few months ago. She doubted her ability to help move the group in a positive and significant direction—even her ability to lead at all. After the pastor empathized with these feelings, the conversation continued:

Pastor: It seems to me that you've been somewhat preoccupied with other things in the last few months. At least, I remember when you led the women's support group, you gave yourself deeply to those women and it was a profound experience for you. So I do not doubt your leadership ability and wonder if this hasn't caught you at a time when you have been dealing with other important matters in your life.

Parishioner: Well, that's true enough. I've been going in more than one direction at a time here lately. That could be it. I hadn't thought of it that way.

Pastor: If it is on target, you have a choice. Either you need to attend to other matters and resolve them, and that's more important for you now. Or you can give a higher priority to the youth program and see if giving more of yourself, as you've done before, makes the difference you want to see.

In this conversation the pastor acknowledged the parishioner's feelings but pointed to some facts that suggest a different interpretation from the one that she had constructed. In doing so he offered an interpretation that was more faithful to the facts than hers. He challenged the woman's potential, though not in a moralistic way.

To confront persons on the basis of their strengths is a guideline that you can apply readily in your own ministry. Reflect for a few minutes on personal strengths that you believe you bring to your ministry. Select one of these and describe it as concretely as you can, jotting down notes that depict this characteristic and suggest examples. Next, ask yourself if there is not some area in your life or ministry in which this strength is underused and challenge yourself to use it in order to grow or to solve a problem you now face. Write out a caring statement of self-confrontation that focuses on your strength, or give yourself a good talking to in front of a mirror. Notice the effect that such confrontation has on you. Reflect on the implications of your feelings for your approach to caring confrontation in your ministry.

Pastors often feel that approaching the subject gradually cushions the blow in a confrontational message. To the contrary, it usually confuses. Talking around a subject in a subtle approach often leaves hearers uncertain: What is the real message? What is the bottom line? Honesty calls pastors to be as brief and specific as possible. After helping a parishioner adjust to several changes and the stress that accompanied these, a pastor talked with him about his new job, a promotion to his first management-level position. They reviewed the strengths that this person brought to the job and a variety of feelings, including anxieties, that he had.

> Pastor: I have one concern, Jim. You have a tendency to give situations their worst reading. While some people are optimists who pretty up things, you look for the worst that can happen. I'm concerned that at times this can affect your ability to lead. How do you feel?

While brief and to the point, caring confrontation is appropriately tentative; that is, pastors must not overstate the case when confronting. To do so is to use the authority of one's office in an oppressive way that frequently short-circuits long-term growth. The question at the end of the pastor's comment above prevented the statement from having a dogmatic tone. Instead, the pastor invited Jim to enter into a joint examination of the pastor's impression. The comment gave Jim feedback on how he comes across, in such a manner that he could own it, if he recognized himself in the description. If not, at least he could explore the matter openly.

As readily as any helping professionals, ministers can help persons relate their decisions to their values. When talking with pastors people often make this connection themselves. At points pastors can raise open-ended questions that encourage persons to explore their decisions as expressions of their values.

A seminary student faced a decision whether to proceed into full-time ministry in the area of the country where he hoped to develop his calling and career, or to locate temporarily where his wife could pursue graduate studies. She had worked to help him through seminary and now wanted to prepare herself for her own career. He fully appreciated what she had done and the importance of her goals. At the same time he recognized that supporting her through school meant deferring the start of the ministry to which he felt called. He chose to help his wife through school, but only after talking over the decision with his pastor, who helped him recognize that though he professed to believe in his wife's vocation as equal to his, he was balking at the limitations this belief imposed on him.

In a conversation with a woman who felt her leadership position with the children's choir threatened, a pastor said,

> You tell me that what really counts in the long run is that the children become a really good choir and learn about Christian faith; yet in most of this conversation you have dwelt on strategies for not resigning but saving face. So I'm sensing that the children's welfare is not the only issue here.

The parishioner moved to a deeper level of exploration in which she faced her ego needs and also took the issue of the children's welfare more seriously than she had previously.

By being confrontive in counseling, pastors encourage and expect persons to examine attitudes and behavior that are self-defeating, manipulative, or harmful to others. That is, pastors raise persons' awareness of attitudes and behaviors that express disrespect for themselves or others. To block gossip in a small group meeting, a pastor said, "I'd like to see us try to limit how much we talk about people who are not here, and concentrate on ourselves." When visiting with a family, a pastor intervened in an exchange between the teen-age son and his father.

Son: I just don't like to get into it with you, Dad.
Father: You think I'm harsh and unreasonable when I don't let you have your way.
Pastor: John, you've said what you assume Brian thinks. Let's hear from him about his hesitancy to talk with you.

Here the pastor confronted the father's tendency to tell other persons what they are thinking, a habit that is manipulative and can destroy respectful communication. Later in the conversation, when the mother asked Brian, "Why do you hide in your room so much of the time?" the pastor said, "Martha, there's some concern, I believe, behind your question. It would help if we could hear it." She went on to tell her son that when she felt out of touch with him she began to worry and also that she felt he was using withdrawal to punish her and her husband, but that she did not know why. Brian was able to respond straightforwardly to her feelings, but probably would have resented having to respond to the question she asked without knowing the concern that lay behind it. Often people use questions in a manipulative, indirect way in order to get at unexpressed concerns. This approach is unfair because it demands that others respond even though the questioner has not taken a position. Pastors' interventions can help people to get past these thoughtless maneuvers in communication.

Though many situations will not change, people sometimes defeat themselves by defining their problems so that they are not solvable. They see themselves as helpless victims. They minimize their own responsibility, telling themselves and others, "I can't," rather than, "I don't." Of course, pastors should avoid the contrary assumption that everything is solvable: that would be a denial of the human condition. Often, the task is to help people come to terms with the limits of life and to do so in a way that foresees constructive possibilites in the future despite the limitations of the present—that ultimately affirms trust in God rather than succumbing to stoic resignation. Yet people frequently misconstrue their situations in self-defeating ways. Pastors can help by challenging these misconstructions. To a college student who had blamed his teachers for his failure to learn, a pastor said, "Though what you experience as teachers' problems may have hampered you at points, you are responsible for your own attitude toward learning. I'm left wondering at this point if you are not letting yourself off the hook by concentrating on their faults."

The initial data for assessing the usefulness of confrontation usually include the effects that a parishioner's behavior has on you. These effects are clues to consider in order to challenge others and yourself. For example, you may find that you are bored as a parishioner talks with you. You may come to realize that this person does not seem to be invested in the so-called problem being brought to you, and you may then wonder about the degree to which this person is assuming the responsiblity to work out the problem. Or you may be impressed with the skills of a person who has almost persuaded you to serve as her advocate but who claims to be unable so to persuade a third party. You may realize that the person's best chances ride on directly advocating her own cause. One key to effective confrontation, then, is your ability to observe carefully your own responses to someone else's communication with you. Were you buoyed by compliments or were you irritated at subtle manipulations? Perhaps you were puzzled by inconsistencies.

Think of your emotional response as a message you are sending to yourself about the parishioner or your relationship. Such a message may be a call to action. What action? In this situation would the action be responsible or impulsive? Consider further the possibility that the other person's behavior is designed to produce the response that you have in fact noted in yourself. However unconscious, is the design destructive? Does it place undesirable limits on your relationship? Does the behavior disclose strengths, graces, and potential that the person is not taking into account?

Keep in mind that your response in part reflects your needs at the time and may not accurately mirror the other person's intentions. Try to avoid projecting your needs onto others. At the same time, ask yourself if you want the kind of relationship and communication that has emerged. For example, you may feel bored and impatient because a person communicates in a flat, uninvolved manner and rambles. It seems to you that such behavior might be designed to keep you from taking the relationship seriously and from becoming engaged significantly in the relationship yourself. Envision concretely the kind of relationship and interaction you do want to have with the person. If your best efforts at empathy and confrontation do not help you move step by step toward such a relationship, probably referral is in order.

In summary, these guidelines are examples of the principle that when confronting others, pastors are called to be respectful. Pastors can be as respectful of others in moments of confrontation as in moments of empathy. This principle helps pastors put into practice what is essentially an extension of what the church fathers called "fraternal correction." Here, however, the primary concern is with personal decisions and Christ-like living, not correct doctrine.

SELF-DISCLOSURE

Self-disclosure occurs when pastors communicate their own feelings and ideas or reveal something about their own personal lives to parishioners. Since it introduces the pastor's own perspective, self-disclosure is very different from empathic listening. Even so, self-disclosure may encourage parishioners to be more open about themselves. Self-disclosure is not necessarily confrontation, but self-disclosure proffers another perspective and so in principle introduces the possibility of one person's challenging another. In the psychological literature self-disclosure refers to any communication in which helpers reveal something about their own personal lives to their clients. The definition offered here is broader. Psychological literature currently debates the pros and cons of counselor self-disclosure. O. Hobart Mowrer and Sidney Jourard are advocates of high self-disclosure.[7] Others believe that counselor self-disclosure may create special problems for working through a transference relationship, may not allow sufficient role distance between counselor and client, may erode a counselor's credibility, and may frighten some clients.[8] In any case the issue of self-disclosure requires additional consideration, since pastors' relationships with parishioners are not confined to structured counseling sessions but entail personal contact in social, educational, administrative, and community settings.

Because of this wider network of interaction, ministers do not find it practical to approach pastoral care and counseling in the image of a helper who maintains a high level of analytical objectivity toward those being helped. For the very reasons that it seems inevitable, self-disclosure places pastors at greater risk than it does private therapists. A personal disclosure that was appropriate in a counseling session may turn up in another area of the pastor's work and impede the reaching of his or her goals. Some argue that, given these considerations, pastors should not do formal counseling with parishioners.[9] To the contrary, when called to help, pastors do well to be aware of what influence they have already had on their parishioners. The task is not how to avoid self-disclosure or counseling, but how to be judiciously selective and make the most of self-disclosure for parishioners' benefit. My main point is that a self-disclosure that communicates a pastor's feelings, observations, and intentions is more important than a self-disclosure that merely reveals personal details about the pastor's own life. My approach does not exclude the latter sort of self-disclosure, but it gives it second place.

Pastors share feelings with simple, brief responses:

I'm distressed to hear that you've been facing difficulties.
I'm puzzled because you say you're angry, but you are smiling.

The latter example also illustrates how pastors may share observations that give feedback to persons. Often it is important to describe clearly the person's behavior and then indicate what effect it has on the pastor:

You have shown a firm awareness of your own feelings, though they have changed. This helps me believe that, given time, you can find a way through these struggles.
You've talked of your husband, then daughter, and your neighbor. I have to confess that I'm missing any connection and am not clear about what you are trying to tell me.

Pastors may state their intentions at the beginning of counseling, but they help clarify their relation with parishioners when they restate their intentions along the way:

My goal is to help you weigh as many alternatives as possible, not to make your decision for you.
You've dealt with some things about yourself here. I appreciate this and want you to understand that I'm still with you as much as ever.

Frequently self-disclosure is helpful as a prelude to a question, and often enough serves one's purpose better than does a question. When it precedes a question, a self-disclosing statement clarifies what is at stake in asking the question. A pastor knew that a couple's relationship had been strained because of differences about role responsibilities in the marriage. He became concerned when they stopped attending worship and other church activities, and feared that this change might signal deterioration in their marital relationship. Reaching the husband on the phone he said, "Steve, I've missed seeing you and Clara lately. I haven't forgotten the tensions you spoke about some time back, and so I'm calling you to ask how things are going for you." Notice that the pastor says something about how he feels and why he is calling. Suppose, instead, that he had said, "I've noticed you haven't been at church lately. What happened?" No doubt the husband would have felt more on the spot because he could not be sure what was behind the question.

To a young man commenting on how his fiancée becomes angry when he is late, a pastor responded, "Can you see why forgetting as an excuse might lead her to think you didn't care?" This is a leading question that functions as a statement. A substitute might be: "Even if from your viewpoint tardiness does not mean that you don't care, it seems understandable to me that she would interpret your being late as thoughtless and uncaring. Can you look at it from that point of view?"

William Oglesby emphasizes self-disclosure of the kind that communicates above all the pastor's intentions. In fact, though philosophically he emphasizes "being" values over behavioral ones, he prescribes what is virtually a behavioral formula in which pastors' responses typically contain two parts: (1) this is what I hear you saying about where you are; (2) in response, this is where I am.[10] I do not recommend that a self-disclosure accompany every empathic listening response, though there may be a rhythmic movement back and forth between empathic and self-disclosing statements. A major consideration is that pastors may come across as too "gray" by not sharing themselves, including their own feelings. Some pastors hold back on sharing their own views because, rightly, they wish to avoid undue influence on people. Yet many parishioners are not about to be intimidated by what pastors say. They look for signs that their pastors experience themselves as equals, not superiors. Self-disclosure often enhances a sense of mutuality in pastoral relationships, even when it introduces elements of challenge. Often persons are helped by such mutuality to acquire the new attitudes and perspectives that are needed to take action or to come to terms with their concerns.

Introducing pastors' own reactions into conversations requires as much discipline as does empathy. As with empathy, pastors need to differentiate parishioners' feelings from their own. Pastors also need to distinguish between what may be an immediate, impulsive reaction and a response shaped by genuine caring and faithfulness to the pastoral calling. The purpose of self-disclosure is not to gratify one's own desires, control others' decisions, or vent frustrations. The pastor's calling and responsibility in relation to parishioners is the primary consideration. One's own perspective can be shared in a way that maintains respect for parishioners as persons and for their perspectives.

Though the primary meaning of self-disclosure as employed here is the sharing of pastors' own feelings, observations, and intentions with the persons they are trying to serve, there is also a place for the kind of self-disclosure that reveals something about one's own personal life. In the introductory chapter Pastor Babcock's reflections about his grief ministry with a widow were discussed. He had begun to doubt that empathic listening was adequate to help this person move beyond a posture of self-pity. It is conceivable that if he had encountered a major loss in his own life, at some point he might have shared something like this with her:

> Though I can't compare my experience with yours, let me tell you that I felt struck down by a significant loss in my life some time ago. Dealing with it was an awful experience for me and a long struggle. Yet there came a day when I felt ready and let go of the heartache. Possibly that time will come for you.

The aim is to plant a seed that may bear fruit at a later time, but not so early that the struggles of grief are denied. The tentativeness in this self-disclosure helps to establish an atmosphere in which another person can freely consider how the perspective may or may not fit.

A few cautions are in order about pastors' revealing their personal experience. Self-disclosure is appropriate when it helps parishioners focus on their issues. At the wrong time self-disclosure distracts persons from facing themselves. When self-disclosure is employed too frequently, it shifts attention inappropriately to the pastor. Naive, uninformed parishioners may misunderstand pastors' self-disclosure. It can disillusion persons who have put pastors on pedestals. On the other hand, it can be helpful when pastors want to set an example of self-acceptance and not idealistic perfection. Persons who have a need to degrade themselves will use pastors' self-disclosure to make a comparison, however distorted, that puts themselves in a bad light. Passive-aggressive persons and gossips may use pastors' self-disclosure in destructive ways outside the personal context in which pastors attempt to be helpful. Generally, the more disorganized the personality of the individual being helped, or the more severe the problems being addressed, the more likely it is that pastors' self-disclosure will affect that person adversely or at least not be helpful. Self-disclosure should not add another problem to an already weighed-down person.

For the sake of mutuality and of confronting parishioners with perspectives on reality beyond their own feelings, pastors do well to be self-disclosing, especially in communicating their own observations, intentions, and feelings. First and Second Corinthians are very strong in this kind of self-disclosure and make a valuable study in this regard. Though sharing stories from one's own life can contribute also to caring confrontation, pastors usually find that limited portions are better than generous helpings!

INTERPRETATION

In pastoral care ministers share themselves and become known as persons. Ultimately, however, it is not the ordinary self that is disclosed in pastoral ministry but Christ. Christ is disclosed, and through Christ, God. No special virtue inheres in self-disclosure except as it becomes a disclosure of Christ in the self. Therefore, the pastor's commitment cannot be reduced to an ideology of intimacy, though pastoral ministry can often be graced with intimate sharing. Pastors are called to give of themselves without exalting themselves or fostering overreliance on themselves. It should not be surprising, then, that there are times when pastors can explicitly point beyond themselves to Christ and the faithful witness of Scripture and Christian tradition. This is to say that there are opportunities for teaching and interpretation in pastoral care. For our purposes, interpretation is any explanation of Scripture or Christian tradition, or any comment that ultimately refers to them. Though pastors may not cite chapter and verse or written source for a theological opinion, the ultimate sources in interpretation are texts. This understanding is informed by Paul Ricoeur's distinction between interpretation and dialogue. He sees interpretation as grounded in reference to texts as fixed objects, such as manuscripts or art objects. Interpretation has constant recourse to the fixed objectness of such "texts." Pastoral care occurs in a dialogical setting, but interpretation of texts is an accepted and vital role in pastoral dialogue.

This understanding of interpretation is markedly different from interpretation as understood psychologically. Pastoral interpretation is not the helping of people to understand their dreams, to make use of altered states of consciousness, or to become articulate about their inner subjectivity. Above all, it is not the teaching of a psychological language that will allow people to gain perspective on their experiences.[11] Pastoral interpretation is the sharing of information and opinions about Christian truth that may assist persons in their celebration and conduct of life. It is spiritual and moral guidance in the inductive, not eductive mode.[12]

There is no question about the importance of teaching in the ordained ministry. The question is, under what conditions do teaching and pastoral care fuse? Most pastors enter the ordained ministry intending to care and hoping that their teaching will express their care. That is, they hope their teaching will be a vehicle for their care.[13] Consequently, for many pastors the opportunity for interpretation is a high moment in pastoral care. This moment can also be the pastor's severest temptation. Sensitive pastors discover that being didactic can interfere with the goal of caring. Does this mean that teaching must be relegated to the classroom? Is it at best a secondary consideration in pastoral care? With these questions in mind, I examine the relation of interpretation and confrontation in pastoral care. Though interpretation can serve various functions, from consolation to confrontation, it has a significant part to play in the task of challenging persons.

I do not believe that interpretation is reserved for corporate worship and the church's educational program. In fact, as Don Browning has explained, moral thinking is the task of the entire church, and is an essential dimension of pastoral care.[14] Still, the difference between interpretation in corporate and individual settings is critical. It is one thing to challenge our unforgiving ways in a sanctuary, where individual dignity is preserved and each one can apply the message as the spirit beckons. It is another to address a text on our stubborn lack of forgiveness to an individual who has come to a pastor for help. Most instances of confrontive interpretation in the Old and New Testaments are directed at groups. When directed at persons, such confrontation is typically addressed to individuals who represent groups, such as the Pharisees. Especially when addressed to persons as individuals, interpretations of Scripture and Christian tradition must be stated so as to challenge the persons without attacking their self-esteem. What safeguards can we employ?

Generally, in the dialogical setting that characterizes pastoral care, there is no need to rely heavily on interpretation. That is, less is more. When the quality of interpretation is solid, there is no need for a great deal of it. This means that usually pastors do not need to interpret constantly, and that when they do they can be brief. No dissertations or exegetical forays that become monologues are needed. If pastors unthinkingly apply the image of the classroom to their personal conversations, they will inevitably explain too much. They do better to limit interpretation to a sharing of information or opinion just sufficient to help individuals struggle responsibly toward practical decisions. In pastoral care the goal is not Christian literacy. The goal is to communicate Christ to people, so that they may hear the voice of Christ speaking in the midst of their celebrations and struggles.

Anxiety can lead to premature interpretation. Typically, interpretation helps people to consolidate gains. That is, an interpretive comment can fortify persons by giving perspective on a decision or confirming a step forward in the person's development. Premature interpretation may sabotage real gains, especially among persons who tend to idealize.

A pastor who used Paul Pruyser's theological themes in his counseling talked with a couple about forgiveness. She did this after they had consulted with her a few times and had made considerable gains in their relationship. The woman had brought their troubles to the pastor after her husband had beaten her. Subsequently, she separated from him and agreed to being reunited only on the conditions that the husband join Alcoholics Anonymous and that they engage in marital counseling. He agreed, and they came to the pastor for help. In the course of counseling, they disclosed at a deeper level the anger they had toward each other. They explored ways to deal more constructively with anger and conflict. They laid plans to reunite, discussed how to prevent recurrences of old problems, and expressed readiness to let go of attitudes toward each other that were outgrown. At this juncture the pastor commented, "Part of what you are affirming here sounds like what Christian faith has called forgiveness." They assented to this interpretation, and the pastor talked with them regarding the nature of forgiveness as both event and continuing process. Her comment both consolidated the gains they had made and kept before them the challenge to continue to exercise the gift of forgiveness in their marriage. Suppose she had introduced this theme at the beginning? My hunch is that it would not have been nearly so meaningful. In fact, it might have produced polite compliance at the verbal level but left untouched their basic resentments toward each other.

Ministers probably understand that many psychological counselors make use of the dynamics of their interactions with persons more than they interpret matters for their clients. Of course, psychoanalysts interpret transferences, and there are a growing number of didactically oriented therapists who teach clients ways to interpret their experience that promote particular values. The approach advocated here calls for judicious and modest use of interpretation. I do not believe, however, that interpretation is secondary to dynamic process. There are points where interpretation strengthens growth because people's intellectual energies are joined with their emotional energies. And there are times when interpretation can help persons move beyond emotional catharsis. The limits discussed above warn pastors against the possibility that interpretation will be used to short-circuit persons' own responsibility to discover meaning. Also, interpretation may defuse the emotional struggles in which persons may need to engage.

In short, ministers do not usually need to be less interpretive than psychological counselors and therapists are. The difference lies in the resources to which they have recourse, even if there may otherwise be much compatibility between the theological and psychological traditions.

Rather than dismiss people's references to biblical stories as of secondary import, pastors do well to respond to them and encourage exploration of them. A parishioner coming to terms with his adultery said that he often felt like David. In exploring this image the pastor helped this person recognize that previously he had identified with the self-righteous always-at-home older son of Luke 15. Now he was in the process of adopting a different orientation, in which the faults of his life and his need of forgiveness were plain, and in which a sense of providential presence continued despite his wrongs.

There are times when pastors have the task of countering misunderstandings and misapplications of Christian faith. At a neonatal center where a premature infant was born with defects, the father rebuked the mother, telling her that the child's handicaps were God's punishment because she had had sexual relations with another man before their marriage. When the woman told her pastor of the incident, he understood that the task was to deal with the marital relationship and the stress of adjusting to being parents of a handicapped child. At the same time he looked for opportunity to help this couple find a more adequate and constructive theological understanding.

Tentativeness in making interpretations is appropriate, just as it is at other moments in the pastoral relationship. A Roman Catholic priest may have the authority of the magisterium behind him, yet there is often much to consider between the general moral principle and the particular situation that a parishioner brings. Protestant ministers frequently understand an interpretation to be a stimulus for inquiry or a hypothesis regarding how a rule applies to a situation, not an authoritative pronouncement. For the sake of mutuality and of confronting parishioners with perspectives on reality beyond their own feelings, pastors do well to be self-disclosing, especially in communicating their own observations, intentions, and feelings. First and Second Corinthians are very strong in this kind of self-disclosure and make a valuable study in this regard. Though sharing stories from one's own life can contribute also to caring confrontation, pastors usually find that limited portions are better than generous helpings!

RELATIONAL CONFRONTATION

Relational confrontation occurs when a pastor explores directly and openly with another person what is happening in their relationship. The relationship between pastor and parishioner is the prime referent. In contrast, general confrontation may address matters that do not pertain directly to the pastor's relationship with the other person. For example, a pastor may confront a person about a tendency to project blame on others. Such confrontation becomes relational only when the person's tendency becomes part of a discussion that focuses on his relationship with the pastor. If the prime referent of relational confrontation is the relationship between pastor and person, the locus is their here-and-now interaction. Typically, the data shared and discussed in relational confrontation come from the way the pastor and person interact with each other, as this is revealed by behavior patterns and attitudes immediately present.

Relational confrontation is especially helpful when pastors are aware of and have feelings about any change in a relationship. The change may be positive or negative, since either may be the occasion for constructive challenge.

In one instance, a pastor's relationship with a parishioner changed when that parishioner came as a representative of a group of persons in the church who wanted to confront the pastor with some of his faults. The pastor listened and thanked him for being honest, and they developed a friendship in which they were able to criticize and support each other more than they had previously done. The pastor was then able to refer to this change in their relationship in order to challenge the person to even greater growth toward straightforwardness and openness in the relationship. In another instance a pastor became aware of an increased distance between himself and a parishioner at the same time that he became concerned about how the person was handling a recent divorce. Relational confrontation was important in order that the pastor could be available to help the person.

Pastors can consider confronting persons about their relationship when conversations become directionless, when they sense tension, resistance, or a lack of trust. Sometimes, for example, a difference in social status impedes open communication. By discussing the difference and attendant feelings openly, pastors often help the person to move beyond the impasse. Frequently pastors are concerned that individuals may become overly dependent on them. Talking directly about the quality of the relationship helps make obvious what is only implicit. There are occasions when sexual attraction needs to be discussed directly in order to assure commitment to a professional and not exploitative relationship. Whenever unverbalized feelings threaten to interfere with open communication, pastors should consider relational confrontation. Robert Carkhuff advises counselors to ask, "What is this person trying to tell me that he/she can't say directly?"[15]

The following guidelines help to communicate respect in confrontive relationships:

1. When beginning to talk directly about a relationship,

pastors should put themselves on the line by disclosing how they feel about the relationship and what they perceive to be happening in it. This is a matter of self-disclosure and is more helpful than opening with a question such as "How do you feel about our relationship?" or "What do you think is going on between us right now?" which leaves the person wondering why the question was raised at all.

2. Even where pastors can be definite about their own feelings, they should be tentative about their perceptions of the relationship, because they see from their own angle and have not yet heard the other person's feelings and observations. At this point tentativeness invites a mutual sharing of their perceptions of the relationship.

3. It is critical that pastors frame their feelings and perceptions in the context of their hopes for the relationship, by letting the person know that the relationship is vitally important and that they have a constructive purpose in mind. The constructive intent behind bringing up an issue in the relationship, or an observation about the relationship, should be stated succinctly and clearly.

4. When addressing a problem in a relationship, pastors do well to own up to their own contributions to the situation. Remembering that it takes two to tango, pastors should describe how they see both themselves and the other person functioning in the relationship. This can help to avoid a tone of accusation.

5. Finally, pastors can invite the other person to share feelings and perceptions about what is happening in the relationship. That is, in addition to the appropriate tentativeness that encourages mutual exploration, pastors should request response from the other person.

A church officer, identified here as Jim, was divorced after he had become romantically involved with another member of the same church. In the aftermath he resigned as a church officer but continued to attend church regularly. His relationship with his minister, here called Pastor Donovan, was friendly, at least on the surface, but the pastor felt that it was not as open as it previously had been. The pastor felt that Jim avoided him, and noted that he never talked about his relationship with the other woman. Jim was reluctant to do anything that put him under the scrutiny of others in the church. He seemed less available to do things with the pastor. In addition to missing the kind of contact they had had, Pastor Donovan felt in the dark about how Jim was coming to terms with the divorce and how he was relating his faith to his life. He wanted to assure Jim of his continued availability as a pastor and friend, and hoped that if the need arose Jim would feel free to call on him. Pastor Donovan arranged to have coffee with Jim and said,

> Your relationship to me has been important to me, and still is, though there has been a change, and I'd like to talk about it. Though we're still on friendly terms, we do not have as much contact as we used to have, and I miss it. That's to be expected since you're no longer an officer, but there's more. Maybe it doesn't look this way to you, but it seems to me that you have avoided me, and I have to confess I've avoided bringing up this feeling. I want you to know, Jim, that I care about you as much as I did before you resigned your church office, and I hope there can be an openness between us so that you'll feel free to call on me as your pastor and friend, and so I won't hesitate to reach out to you. How are you feeling about our relationship?

Notice that the question "How are you feeling about our relationship?" came at the end, not the beginning. The pastor was taking initiative in the true sense of the word, not merely in form. As to self-disclosure, some indication of the pastor's intent is conveyed in the words, " . . . I hope there can be an openness between us. . . ." He highlighted the importance of the relationship and added a brief summation of how he perceived a change in their relationship. He was sufficiently confrontive that he said, " . . . it seems to me that you have avoided me," yet his tentativeness acknowledged that his was an impression only. His admission that he had been slow to express his own feelings about what was developing in the relationship prevented his message from being accusatory. Finally, he invited Jim to respond. All these elements could have been covered in different words. The significance of the considerations raised by Pastor Donovan cannot be captured in pat phrases. Certainly there was more that the pastor wanted to say, but he did not want to say too much before Jim could begin to respond. He kept his opening comment as brief as he could, and left the remainder for the flow of the dialogue that might follow.

When pastors take initiative it is appropriate that they recognize the demands that relational confrontation can place on persons. Many people are not accustomed to direct comments that address the relationship itself. Ordinarily, relational confrontation takes place where privacy is assured, not in a group, unless the group itself is designated as an interpersonal relations, support, or growth group. Pastors have the responsibility of assessing their own and others' readiness for this kind of confrontation. Being sensitive to the demands involved, they owe people the freedom to refuse to pursue the discussion. Oglesby discusses this idea in the context of initiative and freedom.[16] Even so, persons may avoid the question of the relationship itself by sidetracking the discussion to other issues. Here pastors do well to be firm about their intentions and to try to keep the conversation on the relationship itself.

A pastor felt he had a good relationship with a woman on the church's worship committee. The committee adopted a complete plan for renovation of the sanctuary, but the pastor challenged several of the designer's ideas. In response this woman defended the plans in an angry tone and then became somewhat distant. The pastor felt that their relationship had become strained because of this incident and was even reluctant to call another meeting of the worship committee. He appreciated her as a person and as a leader in the church. Her cooperation was important to him because she was very influential among the members of the church. He also was concerned about his pastoral responsibilities toward her, for on two or three occasions she had made passing comments about frustrations with her teen-age daughter. Given the relationship they had had before this incident, he felt that he could bring up his concern that their disagreement about the sanctuary renovation plan and not affect adversely their relationship. At the same time he was prepared for the fact that she well might want to dwell on the particular disagreements between them over the renovation and thus avoid what really mattered to the pastor, having a good pastoral and working relationship with her. He determined that it was important that he make plain to her that he was not out to change her mind on the designer's plans or to challenge her again, but only wanted to reaffirm their relationship and work out any feelings that might stand in the way of free communication between them.

Relational confrontation allows pastors to help parishioners compare their relationship to their pastor with other significant relationships in their lives. It is likely that difficulties in relating to the pastor reflect problems in other relationships. By giving attention to the immediate relationship and working toward its improvement, pastors move to a position of being able to help persons make adjustments in other relationships. Pastors can also help people deal with their relational problems with others, by drawing comparisons with how these persons relate to the pastor. In an example cited earlier in this book, a young pastor met with a couple who planned to be married. In an individual session with the pastor, the groom realized that when he arrived late to see his fiancée he was treating her the way he used to treat his father. At that point the pastor noted that the groom had been late for their meeting. This observation about his behavior in relation to the pastor brought home even more forcefully the behavior pattern the groom was ready to examine and challenge as part of his preparation for marriage.

Relational confrontation produces many significant encounters. Pastors do well to prepare themselves mentally whenever possible by rehearsing how they will initiate these conversations. How people respond, however, is not entirely predictable. Accordingly, pastors find that these conversations call on a wide variety of skills in communicating respect and pastoral caring for persons. In particular, the conversations are opportunities for pastors to show constructive candor, nondefensiveness, and flexibility. The preparation, however, involves not only thinking through how one will begin but an honest assessment of how one feels about the relationship. If pastors do not find in themselves a strong commitment to develop a sound relationship and a realistic hope that this feeling can be reciprocated, they achieve nothing by faking concern or hope.

To apply these guidelines to your own situation, select a relationship, preferably with a parishioner, that you feel has changed in some significant way, and consider the possibility of relational confrontation over this. Formulate your answers to the following set of questions: (1) What characterizes the relationship now? Include any patterns of interaction that stand out in your mind. (2) What changed in the relationship? Does a particular event stand out as a turning point? Here you can compare and contrast how the relationship used to be and how it is now. (3) What significance does this relationship have for you? What is at stake for you should you talk directly with this person about your relationship? What do you hope will be the outcome of relational confrontation? Answering these questions provides you with the data essential for an opening statement of relational confrontation. Rehearse an opening statement in your mind or write it out. This should help give you an imaginative feel for an anticipated conversation, helping you to assess your own readiness for relational confrontation in this instance. Anticipate as objectively as you can how the other person might respond to you. Try to make a judicious decision whether to take initiative in addressing what you see to be problematic in the relationship.

SUMMARY

While empathic listening is fundamental to pastoral work, the pastoral task frequently entails a movement beyond empathy, in that pastors have the opportunity to serve others by challenging their sense of responsibility and stimulating their growth by offering new perspectives for their consideration. The confrontive skills need not contradict the efforts undertaken in the task of listening. This is evident when a common moral bond such as personal respect is embodied in both empathic listening and confrontation. The fact that ministers exert a definite influence on others is obvious when the task of confrontation is considered. Awareness of this influence can help to prevent ministers, morally committed to serve, from manipulating others. Without the moral context of their calling and purpose, ministers do not have ways to distinguish between exerting control over others for various ends and influencing others on the basis of guiding moral principles and pastoral vision.[17] On the other hand, the vision and principles, without embodiment in concrete guidelines, are subject to distortion, and ministers are tempted to think of themselves as better than their behavior warrants. The task of pastoral confrontation calls for a genuine commitment to Christian living on the basis of faith throughout one's lifetime. This means that ministers who would challenge others are open to challenge themselves and to being confronted by others. In this sense one's pastoral care is integrally related to one's personal process of hearing and following Christ. At the same time, one can practice and acquire particular response capacities and initiating skills that help ready one to face particular situations where confrontation is appropriate. These assist but are not sufficient for one's readiness to minister in a given situation. Ministers are responsible for keeping their interpersonal capacities "toned" through vigorous attention to personal contacts and the practice of skills. Such skills derive their meaning, however, not from the fact that they can be learned or that they "work" but from the moral considerations that direct their use. The meaning of confrontation as a core competency, as interpretation, and as self-disclosure in a confrontational context, and the meaning of a particular form of confrontation such as relational confrontation, can be delineated only in terms of the moral implications of God's relation to us in Christ.

Conclusion

Many pastors sense a need in their pastoral care for both empathy and confrontation. They are unsure of a bridge between the two, which in some ways seem to be so different. Some pastors hesitate to confront because they fear hurting others. This feeling, however, often is in conflict with a definite sense of obligation to confront. Frequently pastors are more comfortable with empathy and do not readily move on to try the riskier waters of confrontation. At the same time they regularly come up against the limits of empathy alone and are restless for a way to proceed beyond empathy without surrendering its values. They sense that being confrontive puts them into a very different relationship with parishioners. What are the rules? And, can one move back and forth between empathy and confrontation?

I have not advocated that pastors move beyond empathy in the sense of forsaking emphasis on it and stressing a more confrontational style of relating to people. To the contrary, the first answer to pastors' dilemmas is to gain a richer vision of empathy. In place of stereotyped empathy as wooden responses that repeat what was said, this study has underscored the role of empathy as the communication of respect grounded in the root metaphor of ministry of the Word. Consequently, a cluster of skills emerge as expressions of the empathic spirit, expressions that convey appreciation for a person's worth. Furthermore, the practical guidelines with respect to empathy derive from an understanding of ministry as communication and from the moral value of respect. Empathic pastors do not merely talk about God's valuing of persons. They value persons in their listening to them, and, in listening to them, pastors listen for the gospel coming to expression in their communication and in the pastor's own responsiveness to them. By being empathic, pastors identify with parishioners in their joy and brokenness and listen with them for the Word of grace, and help them to hear and recognize it. The practical guidelines for empathy are not based solely on empirical reports of what works. Rather they are the result of reflection on the meaning of grace and the sacred worth of the person, a worth founded ultimately not on conditions of merit or on the human capacity for self-affirmation but on divine love and mercy.

The project undertaken here, nonetheless, has been more involved than that of enlarging and reaffirming the meaning of empathy in pastoral ministry. I have proffered a vision of pastoral care that encompasses and links empathy and confrontation, clarifies what is morally valid in each and spells out practical guidelines that give expression to moral principles and spiritual vision. In particular, I give emphasis to unconditional respect as the moral principle that discloses the common thread tying empathy and confrontation together. I do not suppose for a moment that it is the only moral link. Yet it effectively displays the integrity of tender-minded and tough-minded love, and thereby demonstrates how empathy and confrontation belong to the same enterprise. At least, *respectful* confrontation and empathy belong together.

Accordingly, effective empathy evokes confrontation. In fact, empathy itself is confrontive in that it calls on persons to listen carefully to themselves and be responsible for their own feelings, perceptions, actions, and decisions. Moreover, since empathic responses help people listen more respectfully to themselves, it promises to help prepare them to listen respectfully to others. When pastors take the initiative in listening to parishioners, they may hope to engage them in such a manner that they will give pastors a respectful hearing. The result can be a dialogical hearing of the gospel.

This means that normally empathy leads to confrontation. Pastors may not always be able to discern to what extent persons' listening to self and to God in response to empathy has been confrontive. Yet pastors usually can sense when personal brokenness has been addressed with grace, and often can identify situations in which confrontation is not forthcoming either as self-confrontation or as a respectful hearing of the pastor. When this is the case, the pastor's attempt at empathy should be reexamined, for ordinarily empathy evokes confrontation. In other words, rather than questioning how to leap from empathy to confrontation, pastors would do well to expect it to occur almost spontaneously and to question what in their attempt at empathy has happened to prevent this movement.

At the same time, respectful confrontation builds on empathy. Again, I see this as a normative expectation. Ordinarily, when pastors confront without being empathic they do not communicate respect. Furthermore, such confrontation usually is ill-informed and relies on the pastor's personal or professional authority more than on a caring attention to the total picture, which includes peoples' experiences as they communicate them, pastors' responses, and perspectives from Christian tradition. There are extreme situations in which little communication of empathy can precede the confrontation that is essential. Even so, effective confrontation assumes that pastors identify with the persons they confront. The first sign of disrespectful confrontation is lack of identity, a spirit that is thankful to God that "I am not like this" person (Luke 18:11).

The moral continuity in the context of ministry of the Word that marks the relation of empathy and confrontation should not obscure the fact that they are different moments in interpersonal relationships. Empathy is the pristine form of pastoral care in its eductive mode. Confrontation is an exemplary form of pastoral care in its inductive mode. Effective pastoral care is ready to make use of both styles, and in many situations true ministry in the name and spirit of Christ involves a balancing of empathy and confrontation that enables persons to transcend their situations. In this process pastors both listen to the Word and witness to it, implicitly and explicitly—verbally, dynamically, and symbolically. This is what is at stake in understanding ministry as communication of the Word when Word is envisioned as a root metaphor. The reality of God's communication can make use of our words but is not limited to human words.

The relationship of empathy and confrontation in pastoral care has been developed through reference to respect. Empathy and confrontation are the twin offspring of a caring spirit.

If this examination of empathy and confrontation has helped pastors to entertain the idea that these forms of caring enrich and complement one another, to anticipate with greater specificity how to be empathic and how to confront, and to understand that becoming a more skilled pastor depends in great part on one's readiness to reflect on the practical implications of Christian moral wisdom, then this study has served its purpose. Pastors can serve people by going beyond empathy. They can do so, however, only by being more faithful to the moral requirements of empathy. If the first sign of respectful confrontation is an empathic spirit that identifies with the other, the last sign is a renewed and deeper empathy made possible only through the mutual journey that confrontation affords.

Notes

CHAPTER 1

1. Avery Dulles, *Models of Ministry* (New York: Doubleday & Co., 1978). See also Bernard J. Cooke, *Ministry to Word and Sacraments* (Philadelphia: Fortress Press, 1976).

2. On basic analogies in the philosophy of science, see Max Black, *Models and Metaphors* (Ithaca, N.Y.: Cornell Univ. Press, 1962); Mary B. Hesse, *Models and Analogies in Science* (New York and London: Sheed & Ward, 1963); and Harvey Nash, "The Role of Metaphor in Psychological Theory," *Behavioral Science* 8 (1963): 336–45. In philosophy and anthropology the following approaches are helpful: Stephen Pepper, *World Hypotheses* (Berkeley and Los Angeles: Univ. of Calif. Press, 1970); Victor Turner, *The Forest of Symbols* (Ithaca, N.Y.: Cornell Univ. Press, 1967); and Sherry B. Ortner, "On Key Symbols," *American Anthropologist* 75 (1973): 1338–46. Though he does not refer to this understanding of metaphor, Seward Hiltner discusses the Word as a metaphor. See his *Theological Dynamics* (Nashville: Abingdon Press, 1972), 166–76.

3. J. N. Sanders, "The Word," *Interpreter's Dictionary of the Bible*, ed. George A. Buttrick (Nashville: Abingdon Press, 1962), 4:868–72.

4. Walter M. Abbott, ed., *The Documents of Vatican II* (New York: American Press, 1966), 26.

5. Don S. Browning, *Religious Ethics and Pastoral Care* (Philadelphia: Fortress Press, 1983), 61–63.

6. Donald Capps, *Life Cycle Theory and Pastoral Care* (Philadelphia: Fortress Press, 1983). On the themes of orientation, disorientation, and reorientation, see Walter Brueggemann, "Psalms and the Life of Faith: A Suggested Typology of Function," *Journal for the Study of the Old Testament*, 17 (1980): 3–32, as well as Brueggemann's *Praying the Psalms* (Winona, Minn.: St. Mary's Press, 1982).

7. Charles H. Cooley, "The Significance of Communication," in *Reader in Public Opinion and Communication*, enlarged ed., ed. Bernard Berelson and Morris Janovitz (Glencoe, Ill.: Free Press, 1950), 145–153.

8. *Webster's New Collegiate Dictionary* (1981), s.v. "communicate" and "munificent."

9. On the concept of intimacy as an ideology, see Malcolm R. Parks, "Ideology in Interpersonal Communication," in *Communication Yearbook Five*, ed. Michael Burgoon (New Brunswick, N. J.: Transaction Books, 1982), 79–107.

10. Philip Rieff, *The Triumph of the Therapeutic* (New York: Harper & Row, 1966).

11. Harry DeWire, *Communication as Commitment* (Philadelphia: Fortress Press, 1972), ix.

12. George Herbert Mead, *Mind, Self, and Society* (Chicago: Univ. of Chicago Press, 1967); see also his *On Social Psychology* (Chicago: Univ. of Chicago Press, 1964).

13. Frederick Sontag, "Anthropodicy or Theodicy? A Discussion with Becker's *The Structure of Evil*," *Journal of the American Academy of Religion* 49 (June 1981): 267–74.

14. Aristotle, *Nicomachean Ethics*, 1103a14–1103b25.

15. James Fowler, *Stages of Faith* (San Francisco: Harper & Row, 1981); Lawrence Kohlberg, *The Philosophy of Moral Development* (New York: Harper & Row, 1981); Erik Erikson, *Identity: Youth and Crisis* (New York: W. W. Norton & Co., 1968).

CHAPTER 2

1. The terms "professional movement" and "field of inquiry" are used interchangeably here. Though movement suggests historic development in the life of church or culture and "field" implies academic discipline, the terms "professional movement" and "field of inquiry" are used interchangeably because the continual influence of one on the other in pastoral care makes them difficult to separate cleanly. Both the development of pastoral practice with its attendant emergence of professional organizations in pastoral care, and the impact of this development on teaching and research in the discipline of pastoral care in theological education are included in the use of "professional movement" or "pastoral care movement." Likewise, when "field of inquiry" or "discipline" is used, pastoral care as a cluster of methods of research, and the influence of this research and teaching on pastoral practice, are included.

2. E.g., Clyde J. Steckel, *Theology and Behavioral Modification* (Washington, D.C.: University Press of America, 1979); Howard W. Stone, *Using Behavioral Methods in Pastoral Counseling* (Philadelphia: Fortress Press, 1980).

3. Howard J. Clinebell, Jr., *Basic Types of Pastoral Counseling* (Nashville: Abingdon Press, 1966).

4. Eduard Thurneysen, *A Theology of Pastoral Care*, trans. Jack A. Worthington and Thomas Wiese (Richmond: John Knox Press, 1962).

5. John B. Cobb, Jr., *Theology and Pastoral Care* (Philadelphia: Fortress Press, 1977).

6. Donald Capps, *Pastoral Counseling and Preaching* (Philadelphia: Westminster Press, 1980).

7. Jay E. Adams, *Competent to Counsel* (Nutley, N.J.: Presbyterian and Reformed Pub. Co., 1972) and *The Use of the Scriptures in Counseling* (Nutley, N.J.: Presbyterian and Reformed Pub. Co., 1977).

8. Martin Buber, *I and Thou,* 2d ed. (New York: Charles Scribner's Sons, 1958).

9. Reuel Howe, *The Miracle of Dialogue* (New York: Seabury Press, 1963), 3.

10. Heije Faber and Ebel van der Schoot, *The Art of Pastoral Conversation* (Nashville: Abingdon Press, 1962), 115.

11. *Ibid.,* 111.

12. *Ibid.*

13. Paul Johnson, *Psychology of Pastoral Care* (Nashville: Abingdon Press, 1953).

14. Victor E. Frankl, *Man's Search for Meaning* (New York: Simon & Schuster, 1970).

15. Carl G. Jung, *Psychology and Religion* (New Haven: Yale Univ. Press, 1938).

16. Three levels of consideration structure this project. The metaphorical level concerns the basic vision of ministry and so gives the project its basic thrust and sense of direction. The conceptual or theoretical level constructs theses that extend the metaphor of the Word in anticipation of practical considerations. The practical level addresses guidance for practice and emerges from the interplay of metaphor, concepts, and reflection on the actual practice of pastoral care. These aspects of structure are separable as "levels" in order to identify various components in the study, yet they cohere and help to define one another. Their relation is not deductive, i.e., one cannot infer by logical necessity the content of one level from that of another.

17. Paul Watzlawick et al., *Pragmatics of Human Communication* (New York: W. W. Norton & Co., 1967), 48–51.

18. T. S. Eliot, *Ash-Wednesday, I.*

19. Cf. Seward Hiltner, *Theological Dynamics* (Nashville: Abingdon Press, 1972), 177–181, where Hiltner discusses the significance of the Eucharist in terms of the most frequent names for it and in light of a dynamic perspective on how it addresses the highest and lowest levels of psychic life.

20. Buber, *I and Thou.*

21. This view is compatible with Stanley Hauerwas's emphasis on characterological virtue. See his *Community of Character* (Notre Dame, Ind.: Univ. of Notre Dame Press, 1981), 8.

22. John Dewey, *Theory of the Moral Life* (New York: Holt, Rinehart & Winston, 1966), 135.

23. For a stimulating discussion of the theme of distance, transcendence, and transference, see Peter Homans, *Theology after Freud* (Indianapolis: Bobbs-Merrill, 1970).

24. Seward Hiltner, *Pastoral Counseling* (Nashville: Abingdon Press, 1949).

25. Stanley Hauerwas, *Community of Character*, 120.

CHAPTER 3

1. *Webster's New Collegiate Dictionary* (1981), s.v. "empathy."

2. Horace B. and Ava Champney English, *A Comprehensive Dictionary of Psychological and Psychoanalytical Terms* (New York: Longmans, Green & Co., 1958), s.v. "empathy."

3. Allen E. Ivey, *Microcounseling*, 2d ed. (Springfield, Ill.: Charles C. Thomas, 1978), 45–78; see also Robert R. Carkhuff and William A. Anthony, *The Skills of Helping* (Amherst, Mass.: Human Resource Development Press, 1979), 31–55; Gerard Egan, *The Skilled Helper: Model, Skills, and Methods for Effective Helping*, 2d ed. (Monterey, Calif.: Brooks/Cole, 1982), 60–61; and Lawrence M. Brammer, *The Helping Relationship*, 2d ed. (Englewood Cliffs, N.J.: Prentice-Hall, 1979), 69–71.

4. Egan, *The Skilled Helper*, 86–99.

5. Ibid., 165–74.

6. *Webster's New Collegiate Dictionary* (1981), s.v. "genuine."

7. Carl R. Rogers, *On Becoming a Person* (Boston: Houghton, Mifflin, 1961), 50–52.

8. Ibid., 62.

9. Egan, *The Skilled Helper*, 120.

10. Romano Harre, *Social Being* (Oxford: Basil Blackwell & Mott, 1979).

11. *Webster's New Dictionary of Synonyms*, s.v. "respect."

12. Don S. Browning, *The Moral Context of Pastoral Care* (Philadelphia: Westminster Press, 1976).

13. On the theme of personal knowledge from a philosophical viewpoint, see Michael Polanyi, *Personal Knowledge* (New York: Harper & Row, 1962).

CHAPTER 4

1. Don S. Browning, *The Moral Context of Pastoral Care* (Philadelphia: Westminster Press, 1976).

2. Donald Capps, *Pastoral Counseling and Preaching* (Philadelphia: Westminster Press, 1980), 33–53.

3. Browning, *Moral Context*, 63–68.

4. Capps, *Pastoral Counseling and Preaching*, 34.

5. Bernard G. Berenson and Robert R. Carkhuff, *Beyond Counseling and Therapy* (New York: Holt, Rinehart & Winston, 1967), 179.

6. Ibid., 178.

7. O. Hobart Mowrer, "Integrity Groups Today," in *Direct Psychotherapy: Twenty-Eight American Originals*, ed. Ratibor-Ray M. Jurjevich (Coral Gables, Fla.: Univ. of Miami Press, 1973), 2:515–61; Sidney Jourard, *The Transparent Self*, (New York: Van Nostrand Reinhold Co., 1971).

8. R. G. Weigel et al., "Perceived Self-Disclosure, Mental Health, and Who Is Liked in Group Treatment," *Journal of Counseling Psychology*, 19 (1972): 47–52; V. J. Derlega, Ron Lorell, and Allan L. Chaikin, "Effects of Therapist Self-Disclosure and Its Perceived Appropriateness on Client Self-Disclosure," *Journal of Consulting and Clinical Psychology*, 44 (1976): 866.

9. Richard L. Krebs, "Why Pastors Should Not Be Counselors," *Journal of Pastoral Care* 34 (December 1980): 229–233.

10. William Oglesby, *Biblical Themes for Pastoral Care* (Philadelphia: Westminster Press, 1980).

11. Paul Pruyser, *The Minister as Diagnostician* (Philadelphia: Westminster Press, 1976).

12. William A. Clebsch and Charles R. Jaekle, *Pastoral Care in Historical Perspective* (New York: Jason Aronson, 1964), 9.

13. On the theme, see L. Guy Nehl, "Nurturing and Mythus Bearing in Clergy Work Motivation," *Journal of Religion and Health* 18 (January 1979): 29–37.

14. Browning, *Moral Context*, 47, 48, 120–122.

15. Robert R. Carkhuff, *Helping and Human Relations: II. Practice and Research* (New York: Holt, Rinehart & Winston, 1969), 93.

16. Oglesby, *Biblical Themes for Pastoral Care*.

17. Ibid., 45–77.